D1600894

# HORRORISM

■

New Directions in Critical Theory

## New Directions in Critical Theory

Amy Allen, General Editor

New Directions in Critical Theory presents outstanding classic and contemporary texts in the tradition of critical social theory, broadly construed. The series aims to renew and advance the program of critical social theory, with a particular focus on theorizing contemporary struggles around gender, race, sexuality, class, and globalization and their complex interconnections.

*Narrating Evil: A Postmetaphysical Theory of Reflective Judgment,*
María Pía Lara

*The Politics of Our Selves: Power, Autonomy, and Gender in Contemporary Critical Theory,*
Amy Allen

*Democracy and the Political Unconscious,*
Noëlle McAfee

# ADRIANA CAVARERO

—

# HORRORISM

## NAMING CONTEMPORARY VIOLENCE

—

Translated by William McCuaig

Columbia University Press
New York

Columbia University Press
*Publishers Since 1893*
New York    Chichester, West Sussex

Originally published in Italian as
*Orrorismo: Ovvero della violenza sull'inerme*

© 2007 Giangiacomo Feltrinelli Editore Milano
Translation © 2009 Columbia University Press

Library of Congress Cataloging-in-Publication Data
Cavarero, Adriana.
[Horrorism : naming contemporary violence / Adriana Cavarero;
translated by William McCuaig.
p. cm. — (New directions in critical theory)
Includes bibliographical references (p.    ) and index.
ISBN 978-0-231-14456-8 (hard cover : alk. paper) —
ISBN 978-0-231-51917-5 (e-book)
1. Terrorism.  I. Title.  II. Series.
HV6431.C38   2009
303.6—dc22

Columbia University Press books are printed on
permanent and durable acid-free paper.

This book is printed on paper with recycled content.
Printed in the United States of America
c 10 9 8 7 6 5 4 3 2 1

References to Internet Web sites (URLs) were accurate at the time of writing.
Neither the author nor Columbia University Press is responsible for URLs
that may have expired or changed since the manuscript was prepared.

# Contents

# Contents

# Translator's Note

**W**ith the author's help I have converted all her references to and quotations from books in English and other languages, for which she regularly uses published Italian translations or translates herself, as well as the many Italian books she cites and quotes in the original, back to the original pagination and wording wherever the original was in English or to a published English translation where I could determine that one existed. In a few cases, I go back to the French or German original and translate the quoted passage into English myself, although there may be a published English translation of which I was unaware or that I could not locate or found inadequate or inconvenient.

The author frequently uses singular adjectives in substantivized form to refer to categories of human beings. An example is *"il vulnerabile,"* literally, "the vulnerable" or "that which is vulnerable." I sometimes leave it as "the vulnerable," but often I translate with a paraphrase such as "vulnerable persons" or "those who are vulnerable." Italian and English have broken the connection between this Latinate adjective and its root word, the Latin noun *"vulnus"* (neuter, despite its termination in *-us*) by using words of different derivation: *"ferita"* in Italian, "wound" in English. The author chooses to restore this link by frequently and deliberately writing the word *"vulnus,"* and I follow her faithfully in this. Readers are reminded therefore that *"vulnus"* is a noun meaning "wound."

The substantivized adjective the author uses most frequently is *"l'inerme,"* which appears in the subtitle of chapter 7, the chapter that also gives the book as a whole its original title and subtitle: *Orrorismo, ovvero della violenza sull'inerme.* In that chapter, she discusses how the meaning of this word ranges from "the defenseless" to "the helpless." I use either option indifferently to translate it wherever it occurs, and I also use the same variation as in the previous example between the naked substantive and an expansion such as "defenseless human beings" or "the helpless individual."

# Acknowledgments

T he theme of this book and the theoretical hypothesis that under-
girds it have their origin in several papers I presented at con-
ferences and public lectures where I was able to garner honest
criticism and precious suggestions. For their intellectual generosity
and for having offered me this opportunity for interaction, I thank
Christine Battersby, who organized the conference "The State She's In"
at the University of Warwick in April 2004; Barbara Spackman, Albert
Ascoli, and Judith Butler, who, in autumn 2004, invited me to deliver
the lectures endowed by the Chair of Italian Culture at the University
of California at Berkeley; and, last but not least, Lino Pertile, who
offered me the same opportunity at Harvard with the conferral of the
De Bosis Visiting Lectureship in spring 2006. Without their encour-
agement and support and without the debate that flowed from these
encounters, I would not have gone on to write this book.

# HORRORISM

# Introduction

### Scenes of a Massacre

**B**aghdad, 12 July 2005. A suicide driver blows up his automobile in the middle of a crowd, killing twenty-six Iraqi citizens and an American soldier. Among the victims of the carnage—dismembered corpses, limbs oozing blood, hands blown off—the greatest number were children to whom the Americans were handing out candy. Did the perpetrators want to punish them for servility toward the occupying troops? Did they think that violence makes a stronger impression when there are no qualms about massacring children?

Mass murderers of this kind give themselves glorious names: "martyr" and "combatant." In the West, they tend instead to be called terrorists. Though the terms are in opposition, both labels imply that the massacre forms part of a strategy or simply a means toward a higher end. If we observe the scene of massacre from the point of view of the helpless victims rather than that of the warriors, however, the picture changes: the end melts away, and the means become substance. More than terror, what stands out is horror.

* * *

Makr-al-Deeb, 19 May 2004. In an Iraqi village not far from the Syrian border, missiles launched by the American forces land on the participants at a wedding feast. Among the forty-five victims there are women and children, as well as a few musicians who had been enlivening the festivities. The high-powered explosives cause an impressive slaughter. Rumor circulates that terrorists had concealed themselves among the guests, but before long it is denied and abandoned. In war, the perpetrators conceded, mistakes happen.

The language of war calls these mistakes "collateral damage," accidents deplored but inevitable. Notable for its breadth, the category of "collateral damage" now extends to cover practically all civilian victims, who, in the overall computation of the dead in Iraq, by now exceed 90 percent. If we observe the scene of massacre from the point of view of the helpless victims rather than that of the warriors, though, the picture changes here too: the rhetorical facade of "collateral damage" melts away, and the carnage turns substantial. More than war, what stands out is horror.

# Names

As violence spreads and assumes unheard-of forms, it becomes difficult to name in contemporary language. Especially since September 11, 2001, the procedures of naming, which supply interpretive frameworks for events and guide public opinion, have come to constitute an integral part of the conflict.[1] One thing is certain: the words "terrorism" and "war" evoke concepts from the past and muddle them rather than give them fresh relevance.

In the discourse of politics and the media, "terrorism" is today a word as omnipresent as it is vague and ambiguous, its meaning taken for granted so as to avoid defining it. Specialized scholarship for its part elaborates wide-ranging systems of classification and sometimes adopts the newer term "hyperterrorism" but basically concedes that it is impossible to define the phenomenon.[2] A similar problem arises with regard to the substantive "war" and the lexical constellation revolving around it. Forget about the terminological weirdness of an oxymoron like "humanitarian war";[3] even the notion of "preventive war" gives rise to well-founded objections, and the expression "war on terror" mounts a direct challenge to the political lexicon of modernity, which, as is well known, reserves the qualification "enemy" for states alone. Equivocal and slippery, the situation is linguistically chaotic. Names and concepts, and the material reality they are supposed to designate, lack coherence. While violence against the helpless is becoming global in ever more ferocious forms, language proves unable to renew itself to name it; indeed, it tends to mask it.

Names obviously do not change the substance of an epoch that has managed to write the most extensive and anomalous, if not the most repugnant, chapter in the human history of destruction. Nor can the crude reality of bodies rent, dismembered, and burnt entrust its meaning to language in general or to any particular substantive. Yet on closer inspection, violence against the helpless does turn out to have a specific vocabulary of its own, one that has been known, and not just in the Western tradition, for millennia. Beginning with the biblical slaughter of the innocents and passing through various events that include the aberration of Auschwitz, the name used is "horror" rather than "war" or "terror," and it speaks primarily of crime rather than of strategy or politics. Of course, in war and terror, horror is not an entirely unfamiliar scene. On the contrary. But this scene has a specific meaning of its own, of which the procedures of naming must finally take account, freeing themselves of their subjugation to power. To coin a new word, scenes like those I have just described might be called "horrorist," or perhaps, for the sake of economy or assonance, we could speak of horrorism—as though ideally all the innocent victims, instead of their killers, ought to determine the name.

* * *

A neologism is always a risk, even more so when it is coined at a scholar's desk. But linguistic innovation becomes imperative in an epoch in which violence strikes mainly, though not exclusively, the defenseless, and we have no words to say so or only those that misleadingly evoke concepts from the past. For that matter, there is a certain novelty, starting with their sex, about our modern mass killers. Women transformed into human bombs and uniformed torturers barely figure in the past. But that doesn't change the fact that a woman, the hideous Medusa, has always been the mythical face of horror. And along with her, the icon of a still more repugnant crime against the helpless, stands the infanticidal woman Medea.

# 1

###### ▬

# Etymologies

## "Terror"; or, On Surviving

*In fact, we often see people collapse in consequence of the mind's terror.*
*It is a simple matter for anyone to infer from this that the spirit is*
*intimately linked with the mind, and that the spirit, once shaken by*
*the mind's force, in its turn strikes the body and sets it in motion.*
—Lucretius, *On the Nature of Things* 3.157–160

The etymology of the word "terror" and the corresponding forms in many modern languages goes back to the Latin verbs "*terreo*" and "*tremo*." Characterized by the root "*\*ter*," indicating the act of trembling, these words in turn derive from the Greek verbs "*tremo*" or "*treo*," which, according to Chantraine, refer "to fear not as a psychological dimension but as a physical state."[1] So, going by the etymology, the realm of terror is characterized by the physical experience of fear as manifested in a trembling body. Significantly, this physical perception of fear, or, if you like, this physical reaction to fear, alludes not just to what we might call the local movement of the body that trembles but also to the much more dynamic movement of flight. Chantraine points out that already in the classical period "*o tresas*" denotes the one who flees. In any case the etymological connection between "*treo*" and "*pheugo*," "to tremble" and "to flee," is well established. On top of that, we have the yet more obvious relationship between "*pheugo*" and "*phobos*" and above all the double valence of "*phobos*," which, as early as Homer, could signify both "fright" and "flight," though its primary meaning is "flight."[2]

Among the many ways of experiencing fear, or to be precise the sudden start of fear called "fright" in English and "*spavento*" in Italian, terror connotes the one that acts immediately on the body, making it tremble and compelling it to take flight. The two states, trembling and flight, are linked but not necessarily sequential. In both trembling and flight, the body is shaking, it vibrates: as though she who trembles in fear were already engaged in flight, or she who flees in terror were logically following up on the act of trembling. The important point, how-ever, lies in what we might call the instinctual mobility associated with the ambit of terror. Acting directly on them, terror moves bodies, drives them into motion. Its sphere of reference is that of a menace to the living being, which tries to escape by fleeing. This menace is directed, substantially, at life itself: it is a threat of violent death. He who is gripped by terror trembles and flees in order to survive, to save himself from a violence that is aiming to kill him.

It is worth noting that in Greek texts the terminology relating to *"treo,"* in particular the substantive *"o tresas,"* is often linked to the domain of war. Signifying a fear of death in battle that is not always the same thing as cowardice, *"o tresas"* indicates the soldier who runs off (*"fuyard"* in French, "runaway" in English) instead of staying at his place in the phalanx.[3] The usage suggests an order, or an ordered disposition, that is broken and con-vulsed by those who flee; in other words, it evokes a turmoil that, although its intensity may vary, finds its maximal figure, one well known to the ico-nography of war, in the disorder of a multitude in flight. It is symptomatic, in any case, that terror, precisely because it belongs to the sphere of instinc-tive movement, is characterized as antithetic to order and control. The cen-terpiece of the terminological constellation that designates fear (*"phobos,"* *"metus," "timor"*), "terror" in this sense displays a specific link with the kind of total fear, synonymous with absolute disorder and loss of all control, known as panic.

The etymology of the word "panic," from the Greek *"panikos,"* leads back to the name of the god Pan, which literally signifies "all" and in mythology designates the god of the mountains and rural life or, more generally, a tel-lurian power that incarnates the totality of the universe. Panic fear, or panic terror, was what the ancients called the feeling of total fear, sudden and unexplainable, caused by the presence of the god. Although for the ancients as well as for the modern psychological lexicon, panic is primarily an indi-vidual experience, it is easy to see why the term lends itself to designating those collective experiences in which terrorized masses flee from natural catastrophes like earthquakes, floods, or hurricanes. Shifting their focus to human violence, the modern social sciences are primarily interested in the collective panic of large numbers of people crowded into restricted spaces. The contiguity of bodies makes masses particularly susceptible to the con-tagion of terror, transmitting and heightening its effects. The individual reaction of flight from violent death is transformed into the collective pro-duction of death itself.

If terror, as its etymology indicates, alludes to fear as a physical state, collective panic is an essential figure of it. You could even say that collective panic brings the physics of terror to complete fulfillment, inasmuch as it forces bodies to turn the very violence that, sweeping them along in the rush of flight, has transformed them into a killing machine against one another.

# Scene

The Shia-Sunni conflict, capable of generating a level of violence that caused thirteen hundred deaths in a single week during the so-called war of the mosques (February 2006) in post-Saddam Iraq, where the ancient rivalries among sects and ethnic groups have been reinvigorated, has also fed on a complex situation in which Islamic-nationalist, jihadist, and Al-Qaeda groups are intervening to increase the extent of the killing. It was in this context that in Baghdad on 31 August 2005, on the occasion of a religious ceremony that brought thousands of Shiites together, the crowd was seized by panic, and almost a thousand people died, either trampled or drowned in the muddy waters of the Tigris. As far as is known, all it took to set off the movement of tremor and flight was a few mortar rounds and above all the rumor of an imminent suicide attack, which agents provocateurs had spread among the crowd. Given the high expectation, objectively well founded, of such an attack, one might even hypothesize that there were no agents provocateurs and that the movement was caused by a saturation of psychological tension stemming from the density of the threat. This does not mean, in any case, that the movement as such can be clearly distinguished from the psychological plane as the causal factor or that it was the mere product of psychology. Rather, in Baghdad, the threat of death was already inherent in the motion of the bodies driven to flight, contiguous bodies prey to panic, bodies captured by the physics of terror, bodies that were compelled to make that threat come true.

# 2

■

# Etymologies

## "Horror"; or, On Dismembering

*O horror! Horror! Horror!*
*Tongue nor heart cannot conceive, nor name thee!*
—William Shakespeare, *Macbeth*

lthough it is often paired with terror, horror actually displays
quite opposite characteristics. Etymologically it derives from the
Latin verb *"horreo,"* which, like the Greek *"phrisso,"* alludes to a
bristling sensation (gooseflesh), especially the bristling of the hair on
one's head,[1] a meaning preserved in the Italian adjective *"orripilante"*
[hair-raising]. This well-known manifestation of the physics of horror
is often linked to another, equally well-known symptom, that of feeling frozen, probably because of the obvious connection with gooseflesh as a physiological reaction to cold, a connection supported too
by the etymological nexus (not established beyond all doubt) between
the Greek *"phrisso"* and the Latin *"frigus"* (cold). Be that as it may, the
area of meaning covered by *"horreo"* and *"phrisso"* denotes primarily
a state of paralysis, reinforced by the feeling of growing stiff on the
part of someone who is freezing. The movement of flight, however,
seems to be excluded, although *"phrisso"* also applies figuratively to
the local motion of surfaces that grow wrinkled, as when the sea is
ruffled by a breeze.

Notwithstanding the tendency noted above to couple it with terror,
horror cannot be inscribed in the terminological constellation of fear
without problems. There is something of the frightful there, but, more
than fear, horror has to do with repugnance. The figure who constitutes the incarnation of horror in Greek mythology bears witness to
that: Medusa, the only Gorgon sister who was mortal. Strategically
located in the myth out beyond Ocean, in the space of the external
and the elsewhere,[2] far more repugnant, with her bristling serpen-

tine locks, than any other monster, she freezes and paralyzes. According to the legend of Perseus—a real autochthonous Greek hero, he—her deadly weapon is her gaze: this points to an affinity between horror and vision or, if you like, between a scene unbearable to look at and the repugnance it arouses. Violent death is part of the picture, but not the central part. There is no question of evading death. In contrast to what occurs with terror, in horror there is no instinctive movement of flight in order to survive, much less the contagious turmoil of panic. Rather, movement is blocked in total paralysis, and each victim is affected on its own. Gripped by revulsion in the face of a form of violence that appears more inadmissible than death, the body reacts as if nailed to the spot, hairs standing on end.

Medusa is a severed head. The body is revulsed above all by its own dismemberment, the violence that undoes it and disfigures it (the English verb "undo," the equivalent of the Italian verb "*disfare*," once had a much more drastic meaning than it does today). The human being, as an incarnated being, is here offended in the ontological dignity of its being as body, more precisely in its being as singular body. Death may transform it into a cadaver, but it does not offend its dignity or at any rate does not do so as long as the dead body preserves its figural unity, that human likeness already extinguished yet still visible, watchable, for a period before incineration or inhumation. Stimulated by the game with mirrors that forms part of the legend of Perseus, many have advanced the hypothesis that Medusa represents the unwatchability of one's own death. As well as being true on the empirical level, this view is easy to defend on the basis of several elements of the myth, among them the petrification of Medusa's victims, which evokes the rigidity of a corpse, and the mirror, which can be taken to allude to the identification of oneself in the death of the other. Yet our repugnance for the severed head is too familiar and spontaneous to warrant the affirmation that this is all there is to it. What is unwatchable above all, for the being that knows itself irremediably singular, is the spectacle of disfigurement, which the singular body cannot bear. As its corporeal symptoms testify, the physics of horror has nothing to do with the instinctive reaction to the threat of death. It has rather to do with instinctive disgust for a violence that, not content merely to kill because killing would be too little, aims to destroy the uniqueness of the body, tearing at its constitutive vulnerability. What is at stake is not the end of a human life but the human condition itself, as incarnated in the singularity of vulnerable bodies. Carnage, massacres, tortures, and other violences even more crudely subtle all fit into the picture. Although the myth prefers to symbolize it with the severed head of Medusa, the repertory that horror reserves for its atrocious scene is ample and articulated.

## Scenes

The chronicles of these times supply us with a few exemplary cases from the repertory of horror. Summoned to identify the remains of his daughter—a young Chechen girl who had blown herself up with an explosive belt—a father declared: "All that remained of my daughter was her head. Her hair was tousled, just as though it had been ruffled by the wind. . . . Apart from the head, all that was left was a bit of shoulder, and part of a finger with the nail. I put everything together into a parcel. All that was left of Ajza was five or six kilos, no more."[3] That the detonation of an explosive strapped to the body pulverizes the abdomen and detaches the head cleanly is a phenomenon well known by now. So is the shambles at the scene of mass killings that makes it difficult to reassemble the scraps of the bodies of the victims, so they may be counted and identified. Given the difficulty of the operation, the limbs of victims and perpetrators frequently get mixed up. The body undone (blown apart, torn to pieces) loses its individuality. The violence that dismembers it offends the ontological dignity that the human figure possesses and renders it unwatchable. More repugnant than any other body part is the head, the most markedly human of the remains, on which the singular face can still be seen.

* * *

The iconography of the French Revolution has made the detached heads displayed to the crowd by the executioner familiar. Despite the repetition of the act, the horrors of the present age break away from the mechanical rationality so prized in the guillotine. Grasping the helpless victim by the hair and standing at just the right angle to the television camera (and thus to the international media audience), the modern executioner slices off the head with a knife. More than simply being carried out, the crime is staged as an intentional offense to the ontological dignity of the victim. Evidently it is not so much killing that is in question here but rather dehumanizing and savaging the body as body, destroying it in its figural unity, sullying it. In an act that strikes at the human qua human, the butchers embrace horror with conviction. As though the repugnance horror arouses were more productive than the strategic use of terror. Or as though extreme violence, directed at nullifying human beings even more than at killing them, must rely on horror rather than on terror.

# 3

## On War

*Homer, here, reaches across history to the very substance of*
*the horror that has neither issue nor redemption*
—Rachel Bespaloff, *On the Iliad*

The etymology of the Italian word "*guerra*" and the English word "war" from the Germanic "*werra*," alludes to a context of fierce combat and disarray. The meaning of the Greek "*polemos*," from the verb "*pallo*," is not dissimilar: what comes to the fore in it is the movement of hurling oneself and of vibrating. The Latin "*bellum*," which strongly evokes a certain type of ordering and lining up in formation, is connected with "*duellum*." But a review of the etymologies does not get us very far in this case. War is a complex arena where the fury of intraspecific butchery reigns, imparting variable forms to the movement of reciprocal killing. That this movement includes terror practically goes without saying. But horror too finds this to be fertile ground.

Embracing them with its intensive violence, war nourishes both terror and horror. The *Iliad* is, in this sense, an exemplary text, starting with the word it uses to designate humans, "*oi brotoi*," "the mortals." As Homer well knows, death is the protagonist of war, in fact violent death that cuts short the lives of young warriors. The essential difference between the conditions of daily existence and those of war lies, for mortals, in the high probability of sudden death, death that occurs through being killed rather than through illness, chance, or accident. War procures an unnatural and bloody death, consigning it to the initiative of mankind and its capacity for murder. In the lucid words of Carl Schmitt, war and its concepts—friend, enemy, struggle—"receive their real meaning precisely because they refer to the real possibility of physical killing."[1] In Homer, this reciprocal homicide presents itself in the form of what, in the first decades of the nineteenth century, Clausewitz could still label "nothing but a duel on a larger scale."[2] The Homeric warriors are duelists, murderers at short range, specialists in close-up homicide in hot blood, the more so in that they kill with the sword. They bear arms and they kill other bearers of arms. Even though the Homeric poems, registering the horror of pillage, also tell of the capture of Troy and the defenseless victims that fall to the Achaean swords, the model of the Homeric warrior entails reciprocal, symmetrical violence, not a unilateral violence vented upon those who are defenseless. Reciprocity, making each one a body open to wounding by the other, is in fact a fundamental principle. "He who strikes is struck, that is the rule," in the words of Pindar.[3] Even Ares, the god of war, he who more than any other immortal displays a vulnerable and scarred flesh, confirms this principle.[4] This certainly does not justify war nor confine it to the "fair play" of battle, but it does allow us to observe terror and horror against the exemplary background of war, understood in the narrow and, as it were, heroic sense of a contest between warriors.

The most celebrated of all warriors, Achilles, is a true specialist in massacre and carnage. "The perfect conformity of his nature to his vocation of destroyer" exalts his "murderous ecstasy."[5] Indeed, Homer calls him perpetrator of massacres, even exterminator of mortals (*brotoloigos*).[6] This word is a combination of "*brotos*" (mortal) and "*loigos*" (destruction, extermination, ruin). Mortal himself, indeed certain that he will die precociously in battle, for that is the bargain he has made with the gods, Achilles, the *brotoloigos*, compels a great many mortals to receive their deaths ahead of time, and violently. The physics of terror starts up in his mere presence. Homeric language is highly explicit and etymologically precise on this point. When Achilles finally enters the fray, the Trojans tremble at the mere sight of him. The whole sequence concerning the advance of the son of Peleus through the enemy ranks, spreading slaughter as he goes, is characterized, even on the lexical level, by a terror that makes his opponents' limbs quiver and drives them to flight. The effect is irresistible: they all quake and flee, including Hector. In the Homeric staging, the role of Achilles in terms of war strategy—the reason for his indispensability as far as the Achaean victory is concerned—depends precisely on this terrorizing effect. Terror convulses the Trojan line, breaks their order of battle, shatters the regular forms of reciprocal violence. Heroes who quake and are capable of turning themselves into "masters of flight" are also to be found in the opposing camp for that matter: "It is a surprising truth of the warrior's universe, where no matter how highly the ideology of valor is prized, it never overshadows the awareness that war and fear are linked."[7] Terror is a part of war; more than a strategic weapon, it is its essence.

But nestled within terror there is horror, like the nucleus of an even more profound and at the same time excessive violence, and it is horror above all that spreads over the scene of war's massacre. The realism of Homer registers all its blood-curdling particulars: guts spilling out of a stomach, the severed head that flies off with its helmet, the spinal marrow that spurts from vertebrae, and Achilles, soaked in blood, driving his filthy chariot over a carpet of bodies. Even understood in the restricted sense of battle between warriors, war is not just an exercise yard in which to give or receive violent death. Nor is this a death that limits itself to cutting off life, leaving the body with its own singular features. Ground-up bodies, limbs torn apart, carnage, and butchery are all part of its habitual theater and render it hair-raising. That Homer describes it for us in detail, proving himself the undisputed champion in the intense representation of the atrocious, depends precisely on his capacity for observing this arena and portraying the repugnant aspect of heroic death. Nor does he overlook the hair-raising treatment reserved for the body of the slain enemy.[8] The maddened Achilles expresses his desire to carve up Hector's flesh and eat it.[9] We are not dealing here with terror but with horror. As Nicole Loraux notes, "in the universe of epic, the wounded body has been penetrated, cut, or torn."[10] If we focus on the unity of the body (given that "the manly body is a body to be opened—according to the rules")[11], so that the vulnerability of the warrior is Homerically exalted, the frame of reference changes. The work of horror does not concern imminent death from which one flees, trembling, but rather the effects of a violence that labors at slicing, at the undoing of the wounded body and then the corpse, at opening it up and dismembering it.[12] Through the ceremony of the dragging of the body tied to the chariot, the offense to corporeal unity actually extends even to the outer surface that is the expression of a unique existence: the face, the physiognomy. There is no more life to rip away from the dead body, only the uniqueness of its figure. Albeit linked to terror by the violence that they share, horror is distinguished precisely in this effect of disfiguration. It goes far beyond homicide, indeed it represents a killing that overshoots the elementary goal of taking a life and dedicates itself instead to destroying the living being as singular body, such that repugnance, as a symptom of a spontaneous rebellion of the body, is, in a certain sense, nothing other than an organic repulsion with respect to the violent act that deforms it.

In the *Iliad* horror also makes an appearance in the guise of its celebrated mythic mask, the Gorgon. The most significant passage,[13] occurring in the so-called battle of the gods, concerns the entry into the fray of Athena, who adorns herself for the occasion. The daughter of Zeus arms herself with a horrendous aegis, at the center of which is the horrible Gorgon's head, surrounded by Phobos (fright), Eris (struggle), Alkè (defensive force),[14] and the dreadful Iokè (pursuit). It is worth noting that the words here rendered by the terms "horrendous" and "horrible" correspond, in the Greek, to vocables related to the family of *deinon*, a lexical item well known for its variety of meanings and difficulty of translation into modern languages. The passage from Hesiod that identifies Deimos and Phobos as sons of Ares often induces translators to render Deimos with "Terror" and, on account of their common root in the verb "*deido*," to suggest that *deinon* too alludes to the ambit of things that terrorize rather than those that are horrible.[15] That the verb "*deido*" implies trembling and flight, as the physics of terror would require, is, however, difficult to maintain. Fear there is, but it appears not to entail movement of the body. The version that, according to a certain philosophical reading, makes *deinon* coincide with a state of displacement totally peculiar to the human being, in particular, with his awareness of the death he cannot escape, appears more interesting, therefore, although not conclusive. In this interpretation, the foreground is occupied by an ontological dimension that insists on the centrality of death. Despite the Homeric choice to call human beings "mortals," however, death is not the focal point of the aegis of Athena. The real focal point, personified by the severed head of Medusa, is rather, and much more traditionally, a horror that curdles the blood and provokes repugnance or a fright that petrifies. On the aegis, a formidable figural synthesis of war, it stands at the center of the composition and determines the circularity of the design. Terror and the whole phenomenology of fear, represented by Phobos and Iokè, are in this sense only gems that adorn it, solid presences but secondary. Primordial nucleus of violence, Medusa looms forth, compelling all attention. The mythic face of horror, she directs back at the warriors the most authentic image of their ontological crime, stripping them of any heroic pretext.

And it is the face of a woman.

# 4

## The Howl of Medusa

*Among the primates probably the deepest and most fundamental fear of all is that of dismemberment, particularly of the severing of the head.*
—Thalia Feldman, "Gorgo and the Origins of Fear"

Medusa belongs to the female gender. We must gaze straight into her eyes, without yielding to the temptation to look away: according to mythology, horror has the face of a woman. In this sense, between the hair-raising monster and Ajza, the Chechen suicide bomber whose head is recovered by her father, there is a disturbing resemblance. Not that the modern champions of carnage, much less those of the past, including the Homeric warriors, are predominantly women. Far from it. As in every theater of violence that we know of to date, men continue to be the unchallenged protagonists. But when a woman steps to the front of the stage of horror, the scene turns darker and, although more disconcerting, paradoxically more familiar. Repugnance is heightened, and the effect is augmented: as though horror, just as the myth already knew, required the feminine in order to reveal its authentic roots.

Obviously the misogyny of the patriarchal imaginary plays a part here. And it doesn't limit itself to Medusa alone. The infanticidal mother Medea, another female figure of horror assigned a place of origin at the far periphery of the Greek world, has accompanied and complemented her for millennia. Between the two, however, there is a species of counterpoint. In the case of Medusa, maternity doesn't enter the picture, or rather it slips in unnoticed, as omission. Medusa doesn't even have a body; she is just a severed head, made celebrated by the so-called *gorgoneion*: the frontal image of her visage that occurs first in the figural art of the Greeks and persists for centuries. Separated from the body, the head of the monstrous woman is also split off from the womb. The stereotype of the female that sees the uterus as the vessel of all ills (as in the example of Pandora) functions in reverse in this case. Through the traumatic dislocation of the maternal belly outside the frame, Medusa, among the mothers of ills, is a sterile mother. She doesn't generate horror nor does she explain why horror should be linked to generation. In her severed head, directly, she incarnates it.

In fact, the hair-raising Medusa is at the same time hair-raised. She incarnates a horror revealed in its effects. The severed head centers attention and condenses the meanings of the symbol. On one hand, it alludes to a violence that, tearing furiously at the body, works not simply to take away its life but to undo its figural unity, to wound and dismember it, to detach its head. On the other, as a head it emphasizes that the uniqueness of the person, which the Greeks located in this part of the body, is being attacked. And since she is always depicted from a frontal perspective, as the *gorgoneion* dictates, never in profile, Medusa is a countenance—in fact "the visage of the living, in the singularity of its features."[1] On the scene of horror, the body placed in question is not just a singular body, as every body obviously is; above all, it is a body in which human singularity, concentrating itself at the most expressive point of its own flesh, exposes itself intensely. The ancient mask, in this sense, teaches us that, even when violence tears at other parts of the body, horror always concerns the face. Or at any rate concerns it first and foremost, given that the uniqueness displayed in physiognomic features is immediately visible and that it discloses itself [*si affaccia*] by exposing itself to the other. The eyes as the windows of the soul perhaps bear this meaning as well.

The legend tells how the hero Perseus—whose name means "he who cuts"—was able, with the help of the gods, to approach Medusa without looking her squarely in the eyes and so to seize her by her hair and cut off her head with a sharpened sickle. The many versions of the myth extant from the fifth century on also refer to the fundamental role of the mirror, which Perseus needs in order to meet the gaze of Medusa in its reflected image without being turned to stone or, in another version, to redirect the paralyzing effect of her own eyes back at her. In this regard, Vernant notes that "when you gaze on the face of the Gorgon, it is she who makes of you the mirror in which, transforming you into stone, she regards her terrible face and recognizes herself in her double."[2] In the myth that tells of the encounter between Medusa and Perseus, the realm of the eye is paramount, whether as the reciprocity of seeing and being seen or, more specifically, as the redoubling and mirroring of the gaze. There is, it seems, a face-to-face aspect to horror that cannot be avoided. As though, in the act of its unprecedented destruction, the singularity of each person were acknowledging itself in the singularity of the other or rather knew that what was being destroyed here was precisely the singular.

The repugnance is shared. The ontological crime that, concentrating on the offense to the human being as essentially vulnerable, makes of wounding a disfiguring and a dismembering is repugnant to the singularity of every body. The mirror games thus become more revealing. It is Medusa who undergoes reduplication, or rather her severed head. The creature sees herself decapitated, and, more precisely, she sees the wound delivered by a mortal blow that leaves her still alive to watch it. In this sense, rather than representing the inhuman as the other—the stranger arriving from somewhere elsewhere—or the hellish grimace of death, or, as Freud would have it, the terror of castration,[3] Medusa alludes to a human essence that, deformed in its very being, contemplates the unprecedented act of its own dehumanization. The quintessence of an incarnated uniqueness that, in expressing itself, exposes itself, the severed head is the symbol of that which extreme violence has chosen for its object. The (specifically) human being is filled with repugnance for this violence, which aims primarily not to kill it but to destroy its humanity, to inflict wounds on it that will undo and dismember it. Nor is this a repugnance that grips the victim of dehumanization alone, the specific wounded body lying at the scene of horror. As singular bodies, the repugnance extends to all of us. Whoever shares in the human condition also shares in disgust for an ontological crime that aims to strike it in order to dehumanize it. The unwatchable is watching each one of us.

Despite the centrality of the eye, to which the legend of Perseus refers, an interesting philological hypothesis about the names in this myth leads in another direction. As Thalia Feldman noted, at the root of the name Gorgon lie several Greek verbs that can be connected to the Sanskrit "*garg*" and allude to the emission of a guttural sound, a howl, a cry not very different from the one warriors emit in battle.[4] Yet more than warriors it is female figures who come to the fore once again. Thalia Feldman mentions Mormo, Baubo, and Gello, creatures of the ancient imaginary, whose role is to incarnate a primitive fear and whose names present an etymological link with verbs related to the acoustic sphere: "to murmur," "to squeal," "to bark." For that matter Medusa is often portrayed with her mouth open. Although the etymology of her name does not lead back to the realm of sound—but rather to the act of reigning or, as a misreading of the ancient mythographers has it, to being unable to be seen (*me idosan*)[5]—Medusa is still one of the three Gorgons. The guttural howl is, for her, a family trademark. Though she does not, as the Sirens do, kill with her voice, the acoustic dimension is part of her essence. That the phenomenon of the voice is inscribed in the female gender, and moreover that it evokes the maternal figure, is well known.[6] Medusa, though, is a woman without a body and without a womb. If she alludes to maternity, she does so obliquely, through absence, loss, negation. The vocal exchanges between mother and child do not belong to her experience, nor does that first peremptory cry of a new life, a baby's first wail. In the severed head, as offense to the corporeal uniqueness of every life, as though it were a citation of the maternity denied to her, the wail of the baby becomes a howl.

The depiction of Medusa with her mouth wide open is not a simple accident, or a secondary adjunct, of her fundamental belonging to the realm of the eye. In fact, eye and voice here encounter each other. The unwatchable, as dismembered body, outraged in its singularity, also occurs as a howl in which the baby's wail, the singular voice of new life, expresses the same outrage. But since we are still dealing with a visual image, this howl is soundless. There is no acoustic vibration, only a wide-open mouth. The extreme cry remains mute. And yet something in this inaudible, frozen, breathless cry is more disturbing to the viewer than Medusa's eyes are. As though, through the characteristic game of mirrors, we, the ones doing the looking, were the ones emitting a soundless howl. Or as though the experience of horror had strangled the cry in (her, our) throat.

## Images

A celebrated picture by Caravaggio at the Uffizi Gallery in Florence portrays Medusa with her mouth opened wide. Rivulets of blood flow from the severed head and mix with the Gorgon's viscous mane of serpents. The staring eyes are not trained on the observer but turned elsewhere, perhaps toward Perseus and his mirror or, more likely, toward that which no one would wish to see. But the focal point of the painting is not her eyes but her teeth, of which we catch a glimpse in her open mouth: bright, sharp, luminous. Behind them looms the faint outline of the tongue: not so much a precise form as the brink of a dark abyss leading to the uvula and the throat. These, however, are unseen. There is only the stain, dark yet deep, of the wide open mouth, a vibrating but soundless shadow. The cry remains mute, strangled. Few other paintings, though, cry out and stick in our throats like Caravaggio's *Medusa*. In its mute resonance, the mirror game is perfect. The horror is revealed without words, without sounds, turning toward an ear frozen in expectation of a howl it will be unable to bear.

\* \* \*

The painting by Edvard Munch known in English as *The Scream* (in Norwegian, *Skrik*, literally "shriek") is equally celebrated. The work exists in many versions, the best known of which is a tempera on wood from 1893, held at the Nasjonalgalleriet in Oslo. Though the author stated that his intention was to represent a cosmic shriek arising from all of nature, the centrality of the wide-open mouth immediately reminds us, albeit through pure analogical suggestion, of Caravaggio's portrait of Medusa. But the reference is oblique, subliminal, more meaningful through the absence of several elements than through their presence. The shrieking figure in the foreground not only is not Medusa but is not even a creature endowed with precise facial features and a sex. It looks more like an ectoplasm with human features, neither masculine nor feminine, whose sexual undecidability is highlighted even more by the smaller figures in the background wearing hats, who by contrast are certainly two men. Nor is this head a severed one. Added to that is the fact that it is completely bald, so that the hair-raising effect of horror, intensified in Medusa, here vanishes. But in place of the hair there are the hands that clasp both sides of the face and model it like a skull, reinforcing the impression provoked by the empty eyes. Thus the analogy is based only on the wide-open mouth, on a shriek that comes to occupy the entire scene, congealing into sound waves that Munch visualizes through undulating lines and curves, violently colored. The effect is that of a Medusa stripped of her mythical substance and clothed in spectral human features, who has lost her hair and her eyes, becoming pure howl—a howl all the more inaudible in that the visual material charged with expressing the waves of sound, as the painter knows well, is mute. And indeed it is precisely this aspect of the painting that evokes the realm of horror, not anguish or desperation, as is often thought. The shriek is here pure and total: howl of all human howls where violence is extreme, where it consummates itself on a being that, dehumanizing itself in the phantasm now stripped of its features, freezes the sonic untranslatability of the outrage on its wide-open mouth.

\* \* \*

Among the photographs taken on the day of the bombings that struck London on 7 July 2005, there is one that seems like a citation of the Munch painting. The shot captures a woman who has a gauze mask on her face, applied by the first aid workers as an initial medication and protection for her facial burns. Her hands are pressing on the sides of her face in order to hold the mask tightly in place. The visual effect is that of a white face in which the eyes are barely suggested by oval cuts that outline empty sockets, while the nose is traced by a thin horizontal line beneath which the opening of the mouth is much more evident. Although we can tell that her lips are closed, the contrast between the apertures and the white surface of the gauze sketches out a depersonalized *gorgoneion*, its most prominent feature the dark opening of the mouth, gaping as though to emit a cry. But it is the resemblance to the painting of Munch, emphasized by the position of the hands, that especially strikes the viewer of the photograph, the more so in that the upper part of the gauze mask covers the woman's hair and makes the figure appear bald. The analogy with *The Scream*, although obviously a matter of chance, highlights a peculiar aspect of the phenomenology of horror. I refer to the correspondence between the impersonality produced by the mask and the impersonality that characterizes Munch's ectoplasmic figure, stripped of physiognomic traits. Obviously any confusion between art and photography must be avoided here. The injured woman is not a pictorial representation or a symbolic icon but a living person, a human being who is suffering in her flesh. She thus reminds us that the violence of horror always hits some one, striking each human victim separately, and that the victims of massacres are always singular creatures, each with a face, a name, and a story. Precisely to the extent that it covers and conceals this individuality, the mask, generic and depersonalizing, takes on a particular significance. It becomes the product, and at the same time the sign, of a violence whose precise aim is to erase singularity. Is that not why the gauze mask—in point of fact a remedy for suffering, a benign medical treatment—howls and materializes the horror of the London bomb blasts even more than the bloodied faces, utterly human in their singularity, captured in other photographs? Is it not for just this reason that it appears, symptomatically, exemplary?

In the photograph in question, however, the woman is not alone. A young man, her rescuer, embraces her. Together they advance: a mask and a face.

# 5

## The Vulnerability of the Helpless

*Insecurity can take many forms, but nothing else plays quite so sharply*
*on our sense of vulnerability. After September 11th we found ourselves*
*in an apparently open-ended and permanent state of emergency.*
—Charles Townshend, *Terrorism*

*. . . a situation in which we can be vanquished or lose others. Is there something*
*to be learned about the geopolitical distribution of corporeal vulnerability*
*from our own brief and devastating exposure to this condition?*
—Judith Butler, *Precarious Life*

Together they advance: a mask and a face. Aligning them, the London photograph makes evident the contrast between a singularity that violence would like to destroy and a singularity not yet offended, that reveals itself in physiognomic features. But they are not simply standing beside each other. There is an embrace, succor, care between them. For the young man, the woman beneath the mask is a wounded singular being. Vulnerable himself, the young man responds to the *vulnus* that has struck the other with his care. Care, medication, the soothing of the wound: the gauze mask is all these things too. Only the context of a bombing that has just taken place could solicit the imagination to mistake it for the mythical icon of horror. Yet the equivocation is not entirely gratuitous. In the ambivalence of the mask, what is revealed is the two poles of the essential alternative inscribed in the condition of vulnerability: wounding and caring. Inasmuch as vulnerable, exposed to the other, the singular body is irremediably open to both responses.

The uniqueness that characterizes the ontological status of humans is also in fact a constitutive vulnerability, especially when understood in corporeal terms. If, as Hannah Arendt maintains, everyone is unique because, exposing herself to others and consigning her singularity to this exposure, she shows herself such, this unique being is vulnerable by definition.[1] Arendt does not dwell on this vulnerability, perhaps because she has little interest in the body. But in emphasizing birth as the decisive category of the ontology of the unique person, she does illuminate the first scene on which the vulnerable being presents itself. Even though, as bodies, vulnerability accompanies us through-out our lives, only in the newborn, where the vulnerable and the defenseless are one and the same, does it express itself so brazenly. The relation to the other, precisely the relation that according to Arendt makes each of us unique, in this case takes the form of a unilateral exposure. The vulnerable being is here the absolutely exposed and helpless one who is awaiting care and has no means to defend itself against wounding. Its relation to the other is a total consignment of its corporeal singularity in a context that does not allow for reciprocity.

In a collection of essays written after September 11, Judith Butler reflects on "the conditions of heightened vulnerability and aggression that followed from those events."[2] Registering the surprise of a country that thought it could not be attacked and condemning a reaction that is multiplying the violence with war and destruction, Butler ponders the possibility of "finding a basis for community" starting from the condition of vulnerability.[3] Her thesis is that vulnerability, understood in physical and corporeal terms, con-figures a human condition in which it is the relation to the other that counts, that allows an ontology of linkage and dependence to come to the fore. In this relational context, to recognize oneself as vulnerable signifies recuper-ating "our collective responsibility for the physical lives of one another."[4] In other words, after the losses of September 11, it signifies moving "the narcis-sistic preoccupation of melancholia . . . into a consideration of the vulnera-bility of others."[5]

From the wound suffered—and perceived as a trauma on the part of a country that considered itself invulnerable—attention shifts to the wound of the other, to the end of recognizing our common condition of vulnerabil-ity. In the historical moment that solicits this reflection, Butler is preoccu-pied above all by the reactive logic of reprisal and revenge, a logic facilitated by the philosophical postulate of an autonomous and sovereign subject that, like the state to which it corresponds, thinks of itself as closed and self-suffi-cient. This is the well-known subject, also called "the individual," that "shores itself up, seeks to reconstitute its imagined wholeness, but only at the price of denying its own vulnerability, its dependency, its exposure."[6] For the pur-pose of "understanding the basis of non-violent responses to injury,"[7] indi-vidualistic modern ontology, refusing to admit dependency and relation-ship, must be radically rejected. In the words of Alasdair MacIntyre, the entire history of philosophy from Plato onward has ignored "human vul-nerability and affliction" and "the connections between them and our dependence on others" in the name of a rational and independent subject.[8] Already inscribed in the birth of philosophical discourse, the illusion of the self-sufficient "I" achieves in modernity merely its best-known and most prominent affirmation. Against this illusion and its perverse political effects, Butler chooses to emphasize that the "I" is not closed but rather open and exposed: "What is prematurely, or belatedly, called the 'I' is, at the outset, enthralled, even if it is to a violence, an abandonment."[9] For the "I" there is at the outset the natal scene, in which the infant is a vulnerable being entirely consigned to the other and thus open to a reply that Butler tends to read in terms of violence. With respect to the category of birth on which Hannah Arendt focuses, the shift of perspective is important. Contemplating the natal scene, Butler holds it important to specify that the relation "by which we are, from the start and by virtue of being a bodily being, already given over, beyond ourselves, implicated in lives that are not our own,"[10] can take the form, in the case of a baby, of an essential need for sustenance, which is however followed by a reply "of abandonment, or violence, or starvation [that gives it over] to nothing, or to brutality, or to no sustenance."[11] The emphasis is thus placed on a vulnerable being who is consigned above all to the *vulnus*, to the wound that the other may inflict on it. That this other, given the setting, is identifiable with the maternal figure is more than obvious. But, perhaps because she is convinced that "there is no reason to assume that these caregivers must be oedipally organized as 'father' and 'mother.'"[12] Butler does not foreground this question.

Thomas Hobbes, a great understander of human violence, examines the same scene and by contrast alludes forcefully to the maternal role. Following a scheme repeated in his major works, he begins by noting that dominion over the child belongs to the mother.[13] The context is a reflection, typical of his age, on so-called paternal dominion; this designation he contests, arguing that it is not the father but the mother who, by nature, has absolute power over the child. Since it is Hobbes we are dealing with, obviously we must take the expression "by nature" seriously. It indicates the state in which mankind finds itself, outside and apart from any political or civil institution. In the case at hand, maternal dominion over children is referred to a setting where there is no matrimony or any other form of contract between the parents. In this natural condition, according to the Englishman, dominion over children belongs precisely to the mother. Not, however, as we might expect—and as the author is at pains to point out—because in giving birth she has given them life but because the very survival of the newborn depends on her: "The title to dominion over a child, proceedeth not from the generation, but from the preservation of it; and therefore in the estate of nature, the mother in whose power it is to save or destroy it, hath right thereto by that power."[14]

Rigorous as always, Hobbes renders the power of generation void, abstracting it from the mother and replacing it with the power of salvation or destruction. Maternal dominion is therefore observed, as it were, from the perspective of the newborn. It is indeed a new life, but above all it is a life totally exposed to others for its own self-preservation, in other words a life vulnerable in the highest degree and, on top of that, defenseless. Indeed Hobbes immediately adds that, "if the mother shall think fit to abandon or expose her child to death, whatsoever man or woman shall find the child so exposed, shall have the same right which the mother had before."

Apparently cynical and pitiless, the logic of the argument is utterly clear. In context, the procreative act does not matter; what counts is an effort to remain in existence, a passion for one's own survival. In utterly Hobbesian fashion, the discourse on the newborn is developed on the basis of a conception of the human being as individual life aiming essentially at its own self-preservation. We must not forget that the author was one of the prime begetters of modern individualism, being in fact the principal conceiver of an ontology of unbinding, the protagonists of which are described as atomized, self-referential subjects, closed on themselves and focused on the desire to keep themselves alive, each at the expense of the other. What unites them in the state of nature—according to the familiar expression *homo homini lupus*—is the fear of violent death, which every man is afraid of suffering at the hands of every other, fear of the war of all against all. So it should occasion no surprise that the mother, as a potential assassin, should also take her place in this general panorama of reciprocal and natural violence. Nevertheless, precisely because of the reciprocity that is missing here, along with a reply that admits violence but also care, we do feel a certain surprise. Not just because, compared to the individualistic ontology of unbinding, the relation between mother and infant winds up being a strange exception but because in this relation the imbalance between the parties is obvious.

Here there are not in fact two, so to speak, equal wolves (born, in a curious and symptomatic Hobbesian expression, "like mushrooms")[15] able to attack each other in turn, as the protagonists of the war of all against all do, in their perfect and symmetrical autonomy. Bound to the other and dependent on the other for its very existence, the newborn infant is not a combatant. Absolutely helpless, although already characterized by its effort to survive, it is vulnerable in a unilateral way. So much so that, to guarantee it any hope of life, Hobbes is forced to attribute to the mother a power over her offspring that, abandoning the generally lupine nature of mankind, plays on the alternative between saving it and destroying it. This is not so much a depiction of denatured motherhood as a drastic revision of the traditional iconography of the maternal, through which Hobbes ultimately supplies us with a perfect figure of the vulnerable being, lucidly presented in accordance with its two essential dimensions: its openness both to wounding and to care.

It is worth emphasizing that, apart from Hobbes and as Butler well knows, it is precisely the thematization of infancy that allows the vulnerable being to be read in terms of a drastic alternative between violence and care. In the case of the biblical story of the sacrifice of Isaac, the alternative assumes a different aspect: the choice posed is between a hand that strikes and one that does not rise to do so. For the situation of the infant, however, the arresting of a violent hand is not enough. It is necessary that the alternative inscribed in its primary vulnerability should also bring into account a hand that cares, nourishes, and attends. That means that the other, incarnated in this scene by the mother, cannot limit herself to the gesture of refraining from wounding. By necessity, the vulnerability of the infant always summons her active involvement. On the other side of care, between the blow that kills and simple abandonment—between infanticide and uncaring—there is thus, in a certain sense, only a difference in the degree of intensity of the atrocity of the gesture. As though mothers who imitate Medea were only at the top of a descending scale.

# 6

### The Crime of Medea

*I who have looked, with these my eyes have seen*
*The children lying lifeless in their blood,*
*Both slain by her who gave them birth,*
*By her whom I brought up, Medea,*
*Since then all other horrors seem mere jest!*
—Franz Grillparzer, *Medea*, act 5

The mythical constellation of horror has a decided predilection for female faces. After Medusa, or maybe even before, comes Medea. The tradition recounts how Medea, reacting to Jason's betrayal, murders her own children in revenge. So Euripides assures us at any rate, for he was the first, in his reworking of the legends about the awesome woman from Colchis, to choose to have Medea commit infanticide.[1] In other versions it is the Corinthians who kill the two children.[2] From then on, among the mothers of death, assassins who only murder their male offspring,[3] "the criminal deed that remains linked, more than any other in the western imaginary, to the name of Medea, is the infanticide of her own offspring."[4] Apart from Euripides' decision, a tragic impulse to commit infanticide is in any case structurally impressed on the mask of Medea or, if you like, on the compulsion to iterate the deed that is typical of the logic of myth. Kerényi describes her as "a cruel sorceress who tore her victims to pieces,"[5] including her newborn brother, Absyrtus, whom she steals from the cradle before fleeing with Jason. In other versions Absyrtus is already a youth, though that does not save him from the barbarous act of his sister, who cuts his body into pieces and throws them into the sea as she flees with Jason and the Argonauts. (It would appear that, in the economy of the story, this is a strategic move to force her father, Aeëtes, to slow his pursuit of the Greek ship while he picks up the pieces of his son in order to give them burial and thus, in a sense, undo the dismemberment.) Insisting on the theme, the legend also gives us the blood-curdling episode that takes place at Iolcos in Thessaly, the first stop on their long flight toward Greece, where Medea compels the daughters of the old king, Pelias, to kill him, cut up his corpse, and boil the pieces in a cauldron. The witch had convinced them that by doing so they would restore their father to his youth. Less gory, although just as atrocious, is her murder in Corinth of Jason's new wife and father-in-law, using her skill with poison. The clever Medea knows many ways of committing murder. In the arc of the story, we encounter in sequence a fratricide; a parricide perpetrated at second hand in which the modality of the crime foregrounds dismemberment; then, in the Euripidean scenario, a murder employing poison that burns the flesh; and finally the cutting of her own children's throats, in other words infanticide by maternal hand, an unusual occurrence. Framed by a misogynist imaginary—very evident in the text of Euripides—this sequence of crimes obviously functions too as an accumulation of excess to emphasize the cruelty of the infanticidal woman. The latter is moreover foreign, savage, and barbarous, as though the crime were so unusual that it must necessarily be committed by a mother who has arrived from elsewhere, from the distant regions of the Caucasus, from those lands beyond the bounds of Greece onto which the infamy of the murder is projected. As though Euripides, a proud standard-bearer of Greekness, could not bear to recognize it in the crimes of Medea, despite that character's rootedness in the "geography of origins," and therefore had to displace them into a "space barbaric and totally other."[6] Speaking through Jason, Euripides is in fact quick to specify that "in all Hellas there is not one woman who could have done it."[7] The murderer of her own children, *paidoleteira*,[8] repeatedly qualified as *deine*, is an outsider who brings her deed of horror from elsewhere. Quite clearly, though, this foreignness is ideologically constructed, fictitious. Indeed it is denied by the chorus, which recalls the infanticidal story of Ino,[9] and also, beyond the Euripidean text in question, by other stories from Hellas that tell of similar crimes.[10]

To project deeds of utmost atrocity onto the outsider is a common but notoriously vain expedient, not least because the mytheme of cutting the bodies of the victims to pieces, inscribed with a certain suspect insistence on the figure of Medea, ends by placing her, without effort, in the most classic phenomenology of horror that Greece transmits to the West. In this sense the kinship between Medusa and Medea, both inhabitants of distant lands, is very close. The dismemberment of the body, canceling its uniqueness and reducing it to flesh without figural unity, is an integral part of the portrait of horror that both inhabit. But in the case of Medea, the icon achieves atrocious perfection. Violence demonstrates here that its aim is to destroy the vulnerable, indeed the helpless, going so far as to undo its corporeal singularity in the early years of life. The victim is not the hero, the combatant at the height of his virility, the champion of reciprocal massacre prepared to suffer *vulnus* on his own body, but rather the infant, the baby. Nor does Hobbes's insistence on sustenance alone, to the exclusion of generation, still hold good. "You could endure—a mother!—to lift sword against your own little ones," exclaims Jason.[11] Centered on the mother, the circle of ontological crime completes itself. She who responds with *vulnus* to the exposure of the vulnerable as the absolutely helpless is also she who manifests a propensity to cut bodies "to pieces," who aims to destroy that uniqueness that every mother immediately recognizes in her child. And the violent response stands out more forcefully because it is from the mother that care is expected.

Generative nucleus of horror, the alternative is always there in the background. The violence consummated on the scene of horror is not pure, not a gratuitous cruelty that could be isolated from the care that constitutes its other face. Care always weighs in the balance, the more so in that it is drastically negated. This is true for every other person to whom the vulnerable being is exposed. But it is all the more true when the role of the other falls to a mother whose involvement is compelled by the absolute and unilateral vulnerability of her child. The icon of the Madonna and child, the representation of a maternality that exalts the sole response of care and comes close to the stereotype of self-sacrifice, is part of the context here. Medea, in appearance at least, occupies the opposite pole. In appearance: because there is also the story of a loving mother—"though you kill them, they were your beloved sons,"[12] Euripides has her say to herself—standing behind the icon of infanticide into which Euripides has made her for millennia. And even if we know that, already in Homeric language, "never is the insistence on the skin's softness so great as at the moment that it is injured,"[13] there is always a melting maternal sensibility in her that notes, as she embraces her sons, "and children's skin is soft, and their breath pure."[14] Though she kills them with a blade that cuts and plunges into their flesh, Medea has nothing in common with the warriors of the *Iliad* and their world. She does not move on the terrain of battle of the *homo necans*. Given that she is a mother, the vulnerable ones whom she terminates with a mortal wound, even at the very moment of the homicidal act, are also recognized by her from a standpoint of care. And it is precisely this "necessary aspect" that makes the violence consummated in this scene a peculiar form of horror that, albeit projected into an other, barbaric space, belongs to the imaginary of the West.

## Scene

To redeem Medea without resorting to the unattainable perfection of the Mother of God, perhaps we might reflect on an episode narrated by W. G. Sebald in *On the Natural History of Destruction*. The scene unfolds in Hamburg, razed to the ground by English airplanes on 28 July 1943, by means of tons of explosive and incendiary bombs that caused a firestorm that "lifted gables and roofs from buildings, flung rafters and entire advertising billboards through the air, tore trees from the ground, and drove human beings before it like living torches."[15] Among the survivors, surrounded by "clumps of flesh and bone, or whole heaps of bodies," there was a woman who succeeded in getting on a train, dragging a suitcase along with her. The suitcase, however, contained not jewels or clothing but the corpse of a baby, her son. In gathering first-hand testimony, Sebald found out that this was not an isolated case: "And several of the women on this train from Hamburg . . . actually did have dead children in their luggage, children who had suffocated in the smoke or died in some other way during the air raid."[16] In its immense desperation, the gesture well symbolizes an absolute, albeit paradoxical, response of care on the part of mothers who found themselves at the center of this horrorist catastrophe. In response to the horror that had befallen those quintessentially helpless—their infants—they took care of them beyond death. That this care was no longer life-giving is obvious. What was looked after, preserved, saved was a cadaver, transported in the moving suitcase-tomb in which the mother had placed that which was dearest to her. Borne away from a horror that the gesture renders somehow even more horrendous and pathetically unforgettable, in the history of ontological crime the luggage of the mothers of Hamburg responds, desperately and from a distance, to the mythical figure of Medea.

# 7

## Horrorism; or, On Violence Against the Helpless

*But it touched my heart so forcibly to think of parting entirely with the child,*
*and, for aught I knew, of having it murdered, or starved by neglect and ill-*
*usage (which was much the same), that I could not think of it without horror.*
—Daniel Defoe, *Moll Flanders*

In the ample repertory of human violence, there is one particularly atrocious kind whose features I propose to subsume in the category of *horrorism*. This coinage, apart from the obvious assonance with the word "terrorism," is meant to emphasize the peculiarly repugnant character of so many scenes of contemporary violence, which locates them in the realm of horror rather than that of terror. Why not simply speak of horror, without going to the trouble of adopting a neologism that may cause some annoyance? A neologism assumes that there exists something new, different, recent. But what is so new about carnage and torture, after all? What is so different about bodies burning under incendiary bombs? What is so recent about the customary, age-old slaughter of the innocents? A simple answer might be that, at first sight and in certain circumstances anyway, what is new is the way in which the massacre is now perpetrated: a body that blows itself up in order to rip other bodies to pieces. And more than that, a female body, as happens ever more frequently; sometimes even the body of a pregnant mother-to-be. Thus the most ancient horror renews itself, reaching the extremity of an axis that originates at its own core. To call it terrorism on the basis that it forms part of a terror strategy of a particularly atrocious kind would be inadequate. Calling it horrorism, on the other hand, helps us see that a certain model of horror is indispensable for understanding our present.

Medusa and Medea are the ancient icons of today's spreading horrorism. Medusa reminds us that the "killing of uniqueness," as Hannah Arendt would say, is an ontological crime that goes well beyond the inflicting of death. Medea confirms that this crime is visited on a body not just vulnerable but reduced to the primary situation of absolute helplessness.

It is worth pointing out that, although the scene of infancy links them and makes them coincide, "vulnerable" and "helpless" are not synonymous terms. The human being is vulnerable as a singular body exposed to wounding. There is not, however, anything necessary about the *vulnus* (wound) embedded in the term "vulnerable," only the potential for a wound to occur at any time, in contingent circumstances. As Saint Augustine said, "the fact that our body in the present moment is not necessarily wounded, does not render it invulnerable."[1] As a body, the vulnerable one remains vulnerable as long as she lives, exposed at any instant to *vulnus*. Yet the same potential also delivers her to healing and the relational ontology that decides its meaning.[2] Irremediably open to wounding and caring, the vulnerable one exists totally in the tension generated by this alternative. As though the null response—neither the wound nor the care—were excluded. Or as though the absence of wound and care were not even thinkable. And yet you might call that indifference, and even bless it, if it were just the absence of wounding, whereas, if it were the absence of caring, we would perhaps have to call it desolation. But exposure to the other that persists over the arc of an entire life renders this absence improbable. In fact, given that every human being who exists has been born and has been an infant, materially impossible.

The infant, the small child—and here lies Hannah Arendt's great intuition concerning the ontological and political centrality of the category of birth—actually proclaims relationship as a human condition not just fundamental but structurally necessary. This means that, as a creature totally consigned to relationship, a child is the vulnerable being par excellence and constitutes the primary paradigm of any discourse on vulnerability.[3] And at the same time and even more so, the primary paradigm of any discourse on helplessness.

As its etymology suggests, the "helpless one" ("*l'inerme,*" literally "the unarmed one") is he who does not bear arms and thus cannot harm, kill, or wound. But in everyday usage, rather than this incapacity to take the offensive, the term "helpless" tends to designate a person who, attacked by an armed other, has no arms with which to defend himself. Defenseless and in the power of the other, the helpless person finds himself substantially in a condition of passivity, undergoing violence he can neither flee from nor defend against. The scene is entirely tilted toward unilateral violence. There is no symmetry, no parity, no reciprocity. As in the exemplary case of the infant, it is the other who is in a position of omnipotence. But albeit exemplary, the case of the infant has a peculiar characteristic that distinguishes it from all other cases: the defenselessness of a baby does not depend on circumstances. In other words, infancy is not a circumstance but a condition, the essential mode in which the human being comes into the world and, for a certain period, inhabits it. Infancy is precisely the span of time, never exactly calculable and in some cases interminable, in which vulnerability and helplessness are completely conjoined. Only subsequently do they split apart. Though she remains vulnerable as long as she lives, from the first to the last day of her singular existence, an adult falls back into defenselessness only in certain circumstances. She is always vulnerable but only sometimes helpless, as contingency dictates and with a variable degree of intensity. That degree is maximal when, as happens in torture, the circumstances that cause a helpless victim to undergo violence are willed, prepared, and organized by armed tormentors.

Having established that vulnerability is a permanent status of the human being, whereas finding oneself helpless—except for in infancy and, sometimes, extreme old age—depends on circumstances, it should be added that the circumstances may vary widely. Sometimes misfortune of a more or less natural kind, distress, suffering, or illness, can make you feel helpless. In such cases, we sometimes say that an adult is as helpless as a baby. The expression is not without a certain tenderness: it hints at a plea for care and emphasizes that the vulnerable one in this case is unilaterally exposed to wounds against which he cannot defend himself. It would be easy, almost a joke, to batter him—which seems to be the thought in the minds of modern hooligans who, for fun, attack persons already ill or debilitated. Atrocious as it is, and worthy to be classified as an episode of everyday horrorism, violence of this type is nonetheless occasional. The helpless person is helpless already. She is attacked but not produced. The scene of torture is different: the situation centered on the helpless victim, far from being a given or a happenstance, is produced artificially or, as the Italian has it, *con arte* ("artfully"). In this sense, torture belongs to the type of circumstance in which the coincidence between the vulnerable and the helpless is the result of a series of acts, intentional and planned, aimed at bringing it about. Several peculiar aspects of horrorism are thereby fully disclosed. The center of the scene is occupied by a suffering body, a body reduced to a totally available object or, rather, a thing objectified by the reality of pain,[4] on which violence is taking its time about doing its work. Death may come at the end, but it is not the end in view. The dead body, no matter how mutilated, is only a residue of the scene of torture. The special form of horrorism of which the torturer is the featured protagonist actually prefers to consummate itself on the living body, to prolong the suffering inscribed in the *vulnus*, bringing the vulnerable one to the limit of bearability of pain and offense. As every torturer knows, the vulnerable is not the same as the killable. The latter stands poised between death and life, the former between the wound and healing care. That the vulnerable one is also defenseless makes things easier, because, since it is unilateral, the violence can unfold as something irresistible, even unlimitable, except that the death of the vulnerable one (her "*venir meno*," in the untranslatable Italian idiom) always does constitute a limit. And this is precisely the limit against which (and not just in the case of torture) horror measures the peculiarity of its crime and, in competition with terror, founds its dominion.

Although it often has to do with death or, if you like, with the killing of helpless victims, horrorism is characterized by a particular form of violence that exceeds death itself. This is starkly evidenced in the infinite scene of torture, a word whose etymological root lies in the Latin verb "*torquere*" (supplying English with the verbs "to torque" and "to distort" and the nouns "torture," "torment," "torque" "torch," and "tort" but normally translated as "to twist"): to torture is to twist and distort the body, to make it into "a body broken to pieces by *tormentum*."[5] But some cases of violent, or even instant, death yield a superabundance of signifieds, in comparison to the simple crime of homicide. Medea is a good example. After all, the celebrated infanticidal mother confines herself to killing the helpless; she doesn't torture them. Though the myth does relate that she tears the bodies to pieces, she does so only after the victims are already dead. Albeit using other means and with scaled-up effects, our contemporary massacres, including those caused by suicide bombers, evoke a similar image. People unable to defend themselves against an unforeseeable attack and hence, in precisely this circumstance, helpless people are killed by explosive devices that often rip their bodies to shreds. Obviously some are wounded as well, which causes the scene to turn particularly repugnant, but not just because we see the "undoing" effect of *vulnus* on a living and suffering body that arouses compassion rather than on a cadaver. Repugnance wells up not so much because of the homicide in itself as because of the offense against vulnerable people who are also defenseless. On top of that, the body of the suicide bomber explodes and is dismembered in the very act of killing, shattering, and dismembering the bodies of others. And, on top of that, this violent body is also, sometimes, that of a woman. The indices of superabundance with respect to the figure of simple killing accumulate and multiply. It is not death, much less the death of the real or imagined enemy, that looms large. The crime discloses its profundity, going to the very roots of the human condition, which suffers offense at the ontological level.

# 8

###### ▬

# Those Who Have Seen the Gorgon

*The intrinsic horror of this human condition has imposed*
*a sort of reserve on all the testimony.*
—Primo Levi, *The Drowned and the Saved*

Although the slaughter of the defenseless is certainly not a specialty of the modern epoch, ontological crime took on new and exceptional proportions in the history of the twentieth century. Between 1915 and 1916 there occurred the genocide of the Armenian people by order of the government of the Young Turks.[1] Massacred in their villages or deported to the Syrian desert to die of hunger, "sent defenseless out on to Asiatic highroads, with several thousand miles of dust, stones, and morass before [them],"[2] more than a million Armenians lost their lives. In the course of the forced march, organized like an ambulatory extermination camp, "every day brought its daily horror, and every day the difficulty increased for the survivors, who dragged themselves forward step by step, increasingly miserable, increasingly gaunt."[3] Old men, women, and children, exposed to an offense that went beyond simple dying, came to an atrocious end through hunger and exhaustion.

Even if the planned massacre of the Armenian citizens of the former Ottoman Empire can be regarded as the prototype of the genocides of the twentieth century, the apex of horrorism was reached toward its middle decades with the Nazi death camps, in which the Jewish dead alone amounted to six million. The list of twentieth-century horrors doesn't stop here. Among other iniquities, it includes the number, as yet unknown, of the victims of the Stalinist gulags and those of Mao's China, to whom must obviously be added the victims of the interethnic massacres that bloodied the ex-Yugoslavia in the 1990s. For many reasons, what has been called the "Auschwitz event" nevertheless remains an emblematic case and, as is often said, a *unicum*. Any present-day reflection on horror must, sooner or later, come to terms with Auschwitz.

In *The Drowned and the Saved*, recounting his internment in the camp at Monowitz-Auschwitz, Primo Levi declares that, as a survivor, "saved," he cannot be one of the true witnesses of the reality of the *Lager*, because he did not touch its depths. The only real witness, whom Levi calls the integral witness, is he who has gone to the heart of the horror. But "those who did so, those who saw the Gorgon, have not returned to tell about it or have returned mute."[4] Those who have seen the Gorgon, are, for Levi, the "drowned," those prisoners "irreversibly exhausted, worn out, . . . close to death" who in the camps were called *Muselmänner*, Muslims.[5] The so-called *Muselmann*, said Jean Améry, another Jewish survivor of Auschwitz, was the internee who "no longer had room in his consciousness for the contrasts good or bad, noble or base, intellectual or unintellectual. He was a staggering corpse, a bundle of physical functions in its last convulsions."[6] Victims of a complete demolition of the human being, the drowned, even though they witnessed everything, were unable to recount it precisely because the demolition consisted of reducing them to human beings who, months before dying, "had already lost the ability to observe, to remember, to compare and express themselves."[7] The reality of the Lager, Levi insists, "was not told by anyone, just as no one ever returned to describe his own death."[8] This is not, though, the obvious muteness that follows physical death. The death of the drowned commences well before their corporeal death. Levi calls them men "in decay," "an anonymous mass, continually renewed and always identical, of non-men who march and labor in silence, the divine spark dead within them, already too empty to really suffer. One hesitates to call them living: one hesitates to call their death death, in the face of which they have no fear, as they are too tired to understand."[9]

Not only is horror confirmed as a peculiar form of violence that exceeds simple homicide; it reveals itself, in the case of the Lagers, as a violence deliberately intended to produce helpless beings paradoxically no longer vulnerable. "Too empty to really suffer," those who have seen the Gorgon represent a degenerated form of helplessness; they can no longer even feel the hurt of the *vulnus* that nevertheless continues to be inflicted on them with methodical perseverance. Confessing that they still populate his memories with their "faceless presences," Levi describes the prototype as "an emaciated man, with head dropped and shoulders curved, on whose face and in whose eyes not a trace of thought is to be seen."[10] The procedure followed to achieve this result, that is, to fabricate the degenerated figure of helplessness known as the *Muselmann*, was technically refined.

The transformation of the prisoners into "miserable and sordid puppets" began as soon as they entered the Lager, with a cruel and incomprehensible ceremonial of humiliation and blows. Then, writes Levi, "for the first time we became aware that our language lacks words to express this offense, the demolition of a man."[11] His stay in the camp, which lasted around a year, not only confirmed his first impression of the inadequacy of language but taught him above all that the demolition of a man articulates itself in many forms before achieving completion in the production of the *Muselmann*. The fundamental principle of the whole project is to instill in the minds of the prisoners "the paralyzing sensation of being totally helpless in the hands of fate."[12] Although the camps may initially have functioned as "centers of political terror,"[13] or, in a more recent definition, as "colonies of terror,"[14] the regime in the extermination camps was not one of terror but rather—as Levi attests—one of horror: a horror that, while presenting itself as absolute violence against the helpless, consisted precisely of the systematic fabrication of its artificial form, perverted and caricatured. The "miserable and sordid puppets" are the upshot of a process of dehumanization that, while always fierce, works initially on prisoners who are still "exposed to insult, atrociously naked and vulnerable."[15] That is, it unleashes its ferocity on the helpless who can still feel the *vulnus*. Invulnerability does not occur in nature; it has to be produced artificially. The established repertory of human savagery is not enough. What is needed are new modes, experimental technologies, unprecedented methods. Symptomatically, though, the outcome of the operation is a paradox. No longer exposed to offense and by now incapable of suffering, the *Muselmann* baffles the very violence of which he is nevertheless the product. Totally engaged in its own destructive passion, violence ends, in the horrorist laboratory of the Lager, by producing victims who can no longer suffer from it.

Many are the scenes of violence and cruelty known to human history. "The Nazi concentration camp system," writes Levi, "still remains a *unicum*, both in its extent and its quality."[16] In the Lager, the system of horror proceeds with methodical persistence; in fact, it begins even outside the gates. Crammed into the sealed wagons headed for the camps, the deportees traveled for days without food or water, amid the corpses of those who died on the way and the screams of those who had already gone mad, forced to meet their bodily needs in public, in buckets that were soon overflowing. Levi emphasizes that this public defecation was "a deep wound inflicted on human dignity" and at the same time "the sign of a deliberate and gratuitous viciousness."[17] And he emphasizes as well how, like the general conditions of transportation in the sealed wagons, this was one of the clearest symptoms of the Nazi will to reduce men to beasts, through a perversion of the difference between the human and the animal. For the latter, defecation in public, far from being a degradation, is natural. For the former, however, it is an explicit instrument in the dismantling of a man, as well as a traumatic wound to his vulnerability, to the vulnerability that stands out more clearly in the helpless one who has not yet degenerated. The manifold degradations to which the prisoners were subjected in the camps, like the nudity, the lice, the bare feet, and the lack of spoons with which to eat their soup, conspired toward the same end. Levi writes: "A naked and barefoot man feels that all his nerves and tendons are severed: he is helpless prey. . . . He no longer perceives himself as a human being, but rather as a worm: naked, slow, ignoble, prone to the ground."[18]

The fabrication of the degenerated helpless person, the ultimate outcome of the whole process, makes explicit use of technologies that work on the sensitive areas of natural human vulnerability. One of many examples of this was the constraint of "public and collective nudity"[19] as a way of rendering ignoble the character of vulnerability that, unlike the animal body, the naked human body on its own naturally presents. If it were just a question of the vulnerable being forced to undergo enormous suffering, however blood-curdling the instrumentarium of the tormentors, we would still be within the confines of the customary scene of horror, characterized by a unilateral violence discharging itself upon the defenseless. In contrast, what lies at the core of the Lager system is a less straightforward violence, one more perversely productive: by means of experiments that surpass in their savagery the known range of cruelty, it is essentially aimed at fabricating a victim, insensitive by now to the *vulnus*, in whom the human dignity of the defenseless degenerates into a caricature of itself.

In this respect, the scant interest of the Lager system in small children is telling. Only a few of these—especially twins, considered particularly useful for medical experiments on human subjects—were regarded as material suited to the work of violence for the methodical fabrication of the perverted helpless. Such fabrication would have been superfluous in the case of children, given that they are the helpless by definition: in other words, they are already, naturally, too close to the end product of the Lager and at the same time, extraordinarily, irreducible to it. The infants born in the camps were killed by a nurse, "often with an injection, while others she strangled or simply threw them into a pail of water."[20] Those who emerged from the wagons were simply sent straight to the gas chambers, as being "parts" unsuited to the exercise of demolition of the human being in which the concentration-camp horror system consisted. As we know from manuscripts hidden by members of the *Sonderkommando* under the ashes of Auschwitz, "six hundred Jewish youths aged between twelve and eighteen years,"[21] although still physically robust and hence suitable for slave labor, met the same fate: the logic of the camp chose to kill them instead of making use of them. One of the differences between the Nazi and the Stalinist Lagers, for that matter, had to do precisely with children: they were not among the detainees in the Soviet camps, not only because it was hard to classify them as enemies of the people but especially because forced labor was the effective purpose of the deportation. On the Siberian taiga too, exceedingly hard labor, performed in unbearable climatic conditions and programmed to lead to exhaustion through hunger and illness, produced thousands of deaths in its daily grind. Those who "hit bottom" in this case, though, were designated by the term "skeletons," being in fact slaves who had "cracked" and who, in a state of "semi-consciousness," led "an existence which had no formula and could not be called life."[22]

Levi writes, with reference to Auschwitz, that the term "death camp" had a double meaning. The simple one refers to the extermination, the organization of mass murder that produces cadavers. The other, more complex meaning refers to the methodical process of annihilation of the human being that has as its result "a hollow man, reduced to suffering and needs, forgetful of dignity and restraint, for he who loses all often easily loses himself."[23] And this was the true purpose of the violent machinery of the Nazi Lager. It largely overrode the economic goal of exploiting the internees as a slave labor force that, in contrast, characterized the Soviet Lagers. As Levi makes a point of noting, at Auschwitz "the outrage motive prevailed over the profit motive."[24] Designed to torture the prisoners and complete their systematic degradation, carried out in conditions of fatigue and atrocious suffering, labor was, in substance, one of the principal instruments of annihilation that structured the logic of the Lagers. The concentration-camp system had an insatiable need for such instruments, ones fit for the purpose of demolishing human beings. Albeit absolutely helpless, the adult who entered the camp was not yet that example of degenerate and perverted helplessness labeled the *Muselmann*. Not yet being a nonman, he still offered resistance, a residual attachment to human dignity,[25] and therefore supplied the process of horror with the kind of material it preferred for the fabrication, within a certain set period, of the "miserable and sordid puppets" who constituted its end product.

One aspect of this fabrication—confirming the fact that, as Levi puts it, "the Lager was pre-eminently a gigantic biological and social experiment"[26]—was the reduction of the prisoner to the instinct of mere survival that calls to mind the Hobbesian figure of the "struggle of each one against all."[27] "One entered hoping at least for the solidarity of one's companions in misfortune, but the hoped for allies, except in special cases, were not there;

there were instead a thousand sealed off monads [*monadi sigillate*], and between them a desperate covert and continuous struggle."[28]

Carefully analyzed by Levi in all their savagery, the various techniques for transforming prisoners into these "sealed off monads" are perhaps summed up by the one most methodically applied: the reduction of the prisoners to absolute hunger. "the Lager *is* hunger: we ourselves are hunger, living hunger."[29] And there is obviously an atrocious coherence between these techniques, aimed at the egoistic atomization of the prisoner, and the final result of the fabrication of the *Muselmann*. When not neutralized by complete insensibility on the part of the miserable and sordid puppets, the human condition of vulnerability entails a constitutive relation to the other: an exposure to wounding but also to the care that the other can supply. If the other responds with violence, those to whom it falls to share the role of victims can, in given circumstances, still count on mutual care, an elementary gesture of pity. The Lager in this respect not only wreaks its savagery on the exposure of the vulnerable to wounding; it creates an unnatural setting for vulnerability as a natural human condition: on the one hand, reducing the prisoners to living hunger in competition for mere survival; on the other, and precisely through this, nullifying any possible relations among them, including the elementary form of relation that is the solidarity of the oppressed. The sealed-off monads concentrating on their own survival, these still-vulnerable helpless ones, are thus already an anticipation of the *Muselmann* who is as indifferent to others as he is to himself. The aberrant final production of the invulnerable makes use of techniques, atrociously coherent, that begin by removing from vulnerability that relational dimension in which it consists. You could even say that the celebrated struggle of all against all depicted by Hobbes, far from being a state of nature, was instead an artificial condition that the Nazi system of horror, vastly exceeding the imagination of the English philosopher, produced in the twentieth century. Rather than wolves, the miserable and sordid puppets are in fact the helpless, no longer even vulnerable, who have already lost any form of relation to their fellows.

Levi recounts that the Russian soldiers who first arrived at Auschwitz on 27 January 1945, to liberate the camp "seemed oppressed not only by compassion but by a confused restraint, which sealed their lips and bound their eyes to the funereal scene."[30] This is the same shame, well known to prisoners, that "the just man experiences at another man's crime; the feeling of guilt that such a crime should exist, that it should have been introduced irrevocably into the world of things that exist."[31] Like many other internees who escaped death, Levi speaks often of another guilt: that felt by the survivors for the simple fact of having survived, for having lived "in someone else's place." Referring explicitly to the guilty deed "committed by another," the shame mentioned above has, however nothing to do with survivor guilt. Giorgio Agamben highlights this acutely, linking it to the fact that "a limit . . . was reached, as if something like a new ethical material were touched upon in the living being."[32] The phenomenon, according to Agamben, has to do with the experience of a subject who has become a witness to "its own oblivion as a subject."[33] This shame, which as Levi states, "the Germans did not know," not only touches on ethics, it also involves the question of ontology. Rather than concerning the subject or the other abstract categories beloved of philosophy, though, it is the singularity of the vulnerable as incarnated body that comes to the forefront of this scene. If Auschwitz is a *unicum* in the long history of human barbarity, if the task of bearing witness to this "Medusa-faced truth" creates a sort of reluctance,[34] that is because ontological crime has here revealed unilateral violence against the helpless to be its decisive criterion. Indeed, through its artificial fabrication of this helpless being—a degenerated helpless one, no longer vulnerable—it has revealed it from the side of the inhuman, of excess. This attests that it is indeed horror with which we are dealing, but, as is often said, extreme, unprecedented, exorbitant horror. What we are dealing with, in other words, is a laboratory in which the essential elements that constitute the twentieth-century version of horrorism, albeit in twisted and aberrant form, unexpectedly cluster together.

In this light, the ample and articulated array of theoretical perspectives that, during the twentieth century, chose to reflect on horror in an aestheticizing vein, often inspired by the sadomasochistic scenario, is particularly disturbing. After Auschwitz, shame, along with repugnance and disgust, are decidedly ill-suited to the disenchantment of pure theorizing. As Levi warns us, to confuse the torturers "with their victims is a moral disease or an aesthetic affectation or a sinister sign of complicity."[35]

# 9

██

## Auschwitz; or, On Extreme Horror

*Over a quarter of a century ago, our lives were interrupted, and doubtless history itself. There was no longer any measure to contain monstrosities.*

—Emmanuel Levinas, *Proper Names*

lthough she did not directly experience the extermination camps, Hannah Arendt provides an analysis of them that accords with Primo Levi's on a few essential points, starting with the conviction that the Lagers, as we read in *The Origins of Totalitarianism*, constitute the final stage of a process that aimed to "dominate man entirely" and annihilate him in a systematic manner.[1] In the Nazi concentration-camp system, "suffering, of which there has always been too much on earth, is not the issue, nor is the number of victims. Human nature as such is at stake."[2] Arendt knows well that universal history is a lugubrious slaughterhouse in which one mass killing after another has taken place, and she does not underestimate the cruelty of which mankind has always shown itself capable. In the case of the extermination camps, however, we are in the presence of a scenario that goes beyond the realm of cruelty, notwithstanding the atrocious suffering of the victims and the pitiless actions of their torturers. This scenario is dominated by an "unpunishable, unforgivable absolute evil which could no longer be understood and explained by the evil motives of self-interest, greed, covetousness, resentment, lust for power and cowardice."[3] What has been called the "Auschwitz event" has to do, in her eyes, with evil in its radical form, not the traditional negative passions of ethics and politics, much less crime and punishment as dealt with in the judicial system. In this laboratory for "manipulating givenness,"[4] it is human nature—in other words, the ontological plane directly—that is concerned.

In *The Origins of Totalitarianism*, especially in the section dedicated to the Lagers, although she often employs the term "horror,"

Arendt does not supply a precise definition of it. She does, though, indicate clearly the ontological node that links the realm of horror to that of radical evil. Above all, she develops a complex analysis that introduces the category of total terror and goes on to specify the point of divarication but also the perverse kinship between terror and horror.

Arendt declared, in a 1953 radio lecture that followed up on her book on totalitarianism, that "terror as a means of frightening people into submission can appear in an extraordinary variety of forms and can be closely linked with a large number of political and party systems that have become familiar to us."[5] In other words, terror is a well-known political instrument employed for purposes of intimidation. This is not to deny, as Arendt is at pains to point out, that it has historically been articulated in different forms and that political science must be able to distinguish among the various "terrorist regimes" with which it has to deal, which may present themselves as institutional powers, revolutionary movements, or small groups of conspirators. Such an exercise in distinction always refers back, however, to a certain conception of terror as a political strategy with precise goals, aiming, in various ways and with greater or less violence, at spreading fear and managing its effects. Political terror belongs, in sum, to the logic of means with respect to ends. It is execrable but not incomprehensible.

Yet in totalitarian violence precisely this logic is strikingly absent. That is seen especially clearly, Arendt argues, when one considers that even totalitarian regimes, before they become such, at their outset, use terror no differently from other regimes, for "the exclusive purpose of defeating the opponent and rendering all further opposition impossible."[6] Real totalitarian terror begins when there is no more opposition to be destroyed or intimidated, when the first stage of ordinary violence is left behind. Recourse to "terror [that] has lost its 'purpose,' that is no longer the means to frighten people,"[7] is in fact typical of totalitarianism. Arendt calls it "total terror," a new category in her already idiosyncratic political lexicon, which she uses to indicate the paradox of a terror that is no longer strategic, because it has departed from the logic of means and ends. This is a kind of terror that is no longer useful, that is indeed counterproductive at the limit, and in this sense, from the point of view of the history of terror, inexplicable.

The inexplicable must nevertheless be comprehended (following the Arendtian rule that comprehension does not mean "deducing the unprecedented from precedents" but "facing up to . . . reality—whatever it may be").[8] In the analytical trajectory of comprehension that has total terror as its object, Arendt thus decides to direct her attention primarily at forms of violence that tend symptomatically to evoke the realm of horror. She draws up a list of historical cases that exemplify the principle that "everything is permitted." In addition to wars of aggression, this list includes "massacre of hostile populations" and the "extermination of native peoples" perpetrated by the colonizers of the Americas, Australia, and Africa.[9] To these examples Arendt adds the concentration camps—but not the death camps—the historical invention of which precedes the advent of totalitarianism. It is telling, however, that, through her brief reference to the scene of massacre, the difficult exercise of comprehending total terror shifts from terror to horror. But the final shift, the approach to extreme horror that characterizes radical evil, requires a further step still: that of going beyond the principle that "everything is permitted" to embrace and activate the unprecedented principle that "everything is possible." That it was possible to manipulate human nature, reducing humans to absolutely superfluous beings, was something that only the infernal laboratory of the Lager could conceive and execute. And it was precisely in that inferno that total terror, meaning terror that has "lost its 'purpose'" and is no longer a tool for striking fear into people, finally came to coincide with the extreme form of horror.

That we are dealing here not simply with horror but with its extreme form emerges clearly in Arendt's text. Life in the extermination camps was such, we read in *The Origins of Totalitarianism*, that "its horror can never be fully embraced by the imagination for the very reason that it stands outside of life and death."[10] As in Levi and the entire literature on the camps, the transformation of the prisoners into "living dead" or "walking corpses" forms part of extreme horror. Indeed, on this point the accord between Levi and Arendt is perfect. She too makes the distinction between annihilation as the simple mass production of corpses and the complex and prolonged annihilation of those who, albeit still alive, are already dead because in them the essential boundary between living and dying has been erased. And it is precisely in this sense that we can speak of the inferno of the Lagers. In Arendtian language, hell is not an overworked metaphor to indicate cruelty and suffering but rather the topos of a traditional imaginary that should be taken literally. It is precisely in hell that no one ever dies. Instead the dead lead a life in which agony is eternalized in a suffering without end. While effective, the comparison only works up to a certain point. In traditional images of hell, the damned retain their individual identities. In the hell of the Lager, by contrast, it is precisely this identity that is systematically nullified.

The collapse of the boundary between life and death is of course a central theme of the literature on the death camps. Already present in books written shortly after the end of the war, for example, the works of Levi and Arendt (although it is Rousset who deserves the accolade of priority), it not only remains at the center of subsequent reflection on the Lagers but emerges as a principal theme in the studies that, inspired in their various ways by Foucault, are today investigating biopolitics.[11] The author of *The Origins of Totalitarianism*, along with others, is often reread in this light, something that is justified by, among other things, that book's ample chapter devoted to racial doctrines. But however legitimate, such a reading is still, in a certain sense, misleading. When the "living dead" are her main topic, Arendt directs her attention to the classic question of ontology rather than to the questions of "*bios*" and "bare life." Even when she reflects on the Lager as a laboratory that manipulates the living so as to erase the discrimination between life and death, the very significance of "death" and "life" are decided on an ontological criterion. Extreme horror, for Arendt, has to do with the human condition as such. It consists precisely in the perversion of a living and a dying that, in the Lager, are no longer such, because they concern a living being understood as "a specimen of the animal-species man" in which the uniqueness of every human being, and hence the necessarily unique dimension of a life that concludes with death, has been annihilated.[12] "The killing of man's individuality, of the uniqueness shaped in equal parts by nature, will, and destiny, which has become so self-evident a premise for all human relations that even identical twins inspire a certain uneasiness, creates a horror that vastly overshadows the outrage of the juridical-political person and the despair of the moral person."[13]

Horror has to do precisely with the killing of uniqueness, in other words; it consists in an attack on the ontological material that, transforming unique beings into a mass of superfluous beings whose "murder is as impersonal as the squashing of a gnat,"[14] also takes away from them their own death. Many were the "methods of dealing with this uniqueness of the human person,"[15] Arendt emphasizes, mentioning the voyage in the cattle car, the shaving of the head, the grotesque uniform, and the "utterly unimaginable tortures so gauged as not to kill the body, at any event not quickly."[16] At the end, all that remained were "ghastly marionettes with human faces" that, like the "miserable and sordid puppets" described by Levi, had nothing more of the human about them.[17]

Arendt describes them as automatons, "transformed into specimens of the human animal,"[18] who behave like the dogs in Pavlov's experiments. But this, she points out, is not an example of the canine species observed in its natural behavior but rather a dog of a perverted kind. The "ghastly marionettes" are indeed perverted with respect to the natural spontaneity that is rooted in the uniqueness of every human being: they are the result of a systematic destruction of the human being that the laboratory of the Lager carries out in order to demonstrate "that everything is possible." The decisive point in Arendt's argumentation is also the most original point in her reading of the extermination. It is a question of the killing of uniqueness as primary ontological crime. And it is precisely on this basis that her reflection can move from radical evil to total terror, retracing the filaments that link them to the extreme form of horror.

Uniqueness, as is well known, is a crucial category in Arendt's thought. Elaborated at the end of the 1950s primarily in the speculative context of *The Human Condition*,[19] it is already present in the book on totalitarianism with a theoretical pregnancy that anticipates its future developments. Here we already find precise definitions that denote it as "the differentiation of the individual, his unique identity" and as the "self-evident . . . premise for all human relations."[20] Even if the language does not yet have the exactness or the complex conceptual articulation that will be developed in *The Human Condition*, the resort to the category of uniqueness—along with the closely connected ones of relation and plurality—performs a decisive function in the Arendtian reading of horror in ontological terms that characterizes the text on totalitarianism. Given her philosophical formation, it seems natural, for that matter, that, in the face of the exceptional destruction of the human being—in the face of this measureless crime that eludes any known measure of crime—Arendt should choose to go beyond the historical plane and solicit, also and especially, the realm of ontology. Indeed, it is precisely philosophy, and in particular modern philosophy, as Simona Forti argues, that Arendt accuses in substance of having executed "an unprecedented attack *on the ontological dignity of the singular being* in favor of the absolutization of the One."[21] This signifies, in Arendtian terms, that the philosophical tradition, just because it ignores the reality of human plurality, ends by fabricating a series of "fictitious entities" whose abstract character does not change even if the names given them do; as epochs and cases dictate, these include *anthropos*, the individual, and the subject. The attack on the ontological dignity of the singular being, while it varies in intensity according to the articulation of the various doctrines, in fact pertains to the speculative method of philosophy as a discipline. To that, rather than to some defect of method, Arendt imputes guilt of the gravest kind: that of representing a point of view for which men in flesh and blood—necessarily unique, particular, and finite—become superfluous.

Albeit presented as a simple error of philosophy, the idea of the superfluity of human beings has in fact shown the capacity to transform itself into a tremendous horror when inherited and put into operation by a certain, unparalleled form of politics. Arendt is very explicit on this point. For her, the horror of the death camps consists precisely in the outcome of a regime that "strives not toward despotic rule over men, but toward a system in which men are superfluous."[22] What philosophy, in sum, had only thought,

Nazism had put into operation. In showing that "everything is possible," the Lager "fabricated" the superfluity of human beings.

In a celebrated letter to Karl Jaspers, dated 4 March 1951, which refers explicitly to the book on totalitarianism but also significantly anticipates the thinking later developed in *The Human Condition*, Arendt asserts that "radical evil" concerns "the following phenomenon: making human beings as human beings superfluous," emphasizing that it is "their essence as humans" that is rendered superfluous.[23] Their humanness is characterized in terms of unpredictability and spontaneity, corresponding to the plurality of human beings that renders each one different from every other. What acts to make men superfluous, Arendt adds, is "the omnipotence . . . of an individual man." And she continues "I suspect that philosophy is not altogether innocent in this fine how-do-you-do. Not, of course, in the sense that Hitler had anything to do with Plato. (One compelling reason why I took such trouble to isolate the elements of totalitarian governments was to show that the Western tradition from Plato up to and including Nietzsche is above any such suspicion.) Instead, perhaps in the sense that Western philosophy has never had a clear concept of what constitutes the political, and couldn't have one, because, by necessity, it spoke of man the individual and dealt with the fact of plurality tangentially."[24]

So while Arendt strongly denies that there is a direct relation between philosophy and the Lagers, she does pinpoint a precise connection between radical evil and the philosophical custom of reflecting on Man instead of on human plurality. To put it another way, radical evil is connected, according to her, to the way in which the philosophical tradition has conceived ontology, not politics. The forms of politics as thought by philosophers are unequivocally different from the totalitarian form, of which the Lager constitutes the essence. As the quoted passage demonstrates, this does not mean that Arendt appreciates or participates in the manner in which philosophers have reflected on politics (given that she in fact accuses them of never having had a "clear concept" of political reality, that is, of having failed to recognize that its essential nucleus—inasmuch as politics is distinct from theory and is, above all, undeducible from it—is action).[25] But it does mean that the linkage with totalitarian evil is not to be sought on the plane of the history of political philosophy. This linkage is to be sought first and foremost on the plane of ontology.

Arendt, like Levi, was among the first to lay emphasis on the novelty of the Nazi horror. That Auschwitz constitutes a *unicum* in the history of violence is an idea now taken for granted in almost all the literature on totalitarian horror, so much so that, to give one telling example, Tzvetan Todorov was able to insist, in a text dating from the last year of the twentieth century, that "totalitarianism was the great innovation of the twentieth century and also its greatest evil."[26] Albeit with different arguments, many authors agree on the *unicum* of the so-called Auschwitz event, including those who, tracing it back to a substantial ineffability, end by attributing to it a Satanic grandeur and thus sacralizing it. Symptomatically, and not entirely wrongly, Arendt's own pages on radical evil are sometimes read in this light.

That her book on totalitarianism, through its richness and complexity, if not its sheer size, and above all through its unsystematic writing style that spills over into narration, should ultimately lend itself to this and many other interpretations is practically inevitable. On top of that, Arendt herself recognized and stated the risks inherent in emphasizing the radicality of evil; it is well known that she reconsidered her own position.[27] The work on totalitarianism retains its stature, however, as an analysis of great speculative originality, in which, in the face of the historical irruption of the unheard-of, the main categories of the lexicon of violence were isolated, distinguished, and discussed: terror, evil, horror. Crucially though, Arendtian language attaches the qualifications "total" and "radical" only to the first two terms. Though Arendt portrays it as extreme, horror nevertheless remains without adjectives, as if no further specification were necessary to reveal the whole abyss of its perversion. As if horror, in the constitutive measurelessness of its ontological crime, were sufficient unto itself.

It should be noted as well that in *The Origins of Totalitarianism* this ontological crime is visited upon a human being of whom the uniqueness but not the vulnerability is highlighted. Contrary to what she will later write in *The Human Condition*, the unique being the laboratory of the Lager annihilates by transforming it into an "exemplar" of the species, albeit already characterized by plurality and relation, is not yet the one exposed to the other and thus the vulnerable. The helpless one stands at the center of the scene, indeed he shows all the signs of his atrocious perversion by the concentration-camp machinery, but he does not rise explicitly to the status of criterion of horror. In this sense, in his comprehension of the horrorism of which Auschwitz constitutes the unrivaled paradigm, Levi goes further than Arendt. As does Rousset, another witness whom Arendt often cites but does not, perhaps, entirely comprehend.

# 10

###### ■

## Erotic Carnages

*Throughout the century, cruelty has been less a moral question
than an aesthetic one. . . . Ultimately, cruelty is the moment
when the integral dissolution of the "I" must be decided.*
—Alain Badiou, *The Century*

rendt called David Rousset's *Les jours de notre mort*, published at
Paris in 1947, one of the "best reports on Nazi concentration
camps."[1] She frequently refers to this first-hand testimony, from
which she derives not just the theme of living corpses and the figure of
inferno but especially the description of the internees as "agitated and
grotesque mannequins," in whom it is not difficult to recognize the
"ghastly marionettes." One sentence of Rousset's, which appears several times in Arendt's text and is crucial to its architecture, also appears
as an epigraph to part three of the book, specifically entitled "Totalitarianism." It states: "Normal men do not know that everything is possible." "The extent of character transformation,"[2] the reduction of a
human being to the status of mere exemplar of the human species,
simply cannot be conceived by normal men who do not know that
"everything is possible." A survivor of Buchenwald, the political prisoner David Rousset was forced to shed this ignorance, and for Arendt
this gave him the power to identify the operative principle of what she
calls radical evil and thus the ontological dimension of horror.

In *The Origins of Totalitarianism*, the quotations from Rousset do
grow more frequent whenever the focus shifts to the theme of horror.
Yet alongside her explicit appreciation for the French writer, Arendt
also develops in these pages, as readers can easily detect, a polemical
discourse that is indirect and strangely reticent. An example is the
absence of any explicit reference to Rousset when Arendt argues
strongly against the view that the experience of the internees could
"become the basis of a political community."[3] This is Rousset's explicit

thesis and is in fact the main reason his reflections on the concentration-camp universe differ from those of other relevant witnesses.[4] This polemical strategy, which prefers reticence, reaches its most curious point in a brief, almost hermetic observation in which Arendt directs her criticism at one of the most alert readers of Rousset, Georges Bataille, who had promptly reviewed *Les jours de notre mort* in *Critique* in 1947. Arendt accuses Bataille of "think[ing] it 'superficial' to 'dwell on horrors.'"[5] In Arendt's text, this accusation is expressed in rather unclear and imprecise terms, which a reading of Bataille's text shows to be unjustified. (It may be that here, as elsewhere, Arendt was quoting from memory.) The crucial point in any case is that Bataille functions as the target of a rather murky polemic, that would appear to concern Rousset instead. In other words, it turns out to be crucial that, in the context of a strangely reticent criticism directed at Rousset's fundamental thesis, Arendt's reflections on horror intersect, however briefly, with those of Bataille.

It is worth repeating that in the specific context of Arendt's argumentation, the reference to Bataille occupies no more than a few difficult-to-decipher lines that would merit little notice if not for the importance of the writer whom they challenge. Bataille influenced many of the protagonists of contemporary French thought; not only does he occupy a leading position among the "damned" philosophers of the twentieth century, he is still one of the points of reference for a certain mode of thinking about horror that tends to emphasize, if not relish, its erotic aspects. We are dealing here with an important theoretical stance, the incidence and pressure of which on the modern debate on violence is, to say the least, notable. Inclined to eroticize horror, or, if one prefers, to horrify eros, and often centered on psychoanalytic categories that in Bataille bore less weight, this debate not only flourishes legitimately in disciplinary sectors of varied derivation, it directly involves the mass culture of horror and cheap pornography.

In *The Origins of Totalitarianism*, Arendt not only cites Bataille's review of Rousset, she also mentions his essays on Sade.[6] These are the essays, now famous, which feature a reading of horror centered on "the possibilities of destroying human beings, of destroying them and delighting in the thought of their death and their suffering."[7] The writings of Sade, who "knew that he was going as far as it is imaginable to go," Bataille adds tellingly, "give this sensation: that with an exasperated resolution, he desired *the impossible* and the *underside* of life."[8] Sexual frenzy, especially in its criminal form, has the merit of "decomposing the coherent figures that we establish, for ourselves and for others, inasmuch as they are definite beings (it already impels them into an infinite, which is death)."[9] And for that matter it is precisely this dissolution of the finite into the infinite, erotically enjoyed in cruelty, that solicits Bataille's interest in Sade, who remained one of his principal points of reference.

The Bataille cited by Arendt—the reviewer of Rousset and above all the essayist on Sade—had in any case already elaborated the decisive elements of his thesis on the voluptuous overlap of death and eros, which went into his book *Eroticism* and later into the blood-curdling museum of horrors entitle *The Tears of Eros*. In particular, he had already laid the basis for his conception of the "sovereign" subject as he who, in contrast to the servile subject, does not follow the (bourgeois) principles of utility and self-preservation but rather those of loss and self-destruction, experiencing full erotic inebriation. That Arendt shows no enthusiasm for his ideas thus arouses no surprise.

The reference to Bataille's essays on Sade appears, without comment, in a note in which Arendt signals that, from around 1930, a certain literary avant-garde began to develop a predilection for seeking the sublime in the infamous.[10] The context is her reflection on "the antihumanist, antiliberal, anti-individualist, and anticultural instincts of the front generation," which had "elevated cruelty to a major virtue."[11] More generally, Arendt is here trying to isolate the linkage between the sacrificeability of the self that characterizes mass man in totalitarian regimes and the "yearning for 'losing their selves'" that the generation of the front, meaning the one mobilized in the First World War, had already manifested.[12] Although Arendt mentions him elsewhere for his anti-Semitic writings,[13] one thinks here of the autobiographical Céline of *Voyage to the End of the Night* (which was published in 1932 and immediately achieved worldwide literary success), in which enrollment for the front is described as "lining up to go off and get killed," in a world in which "everything has shrunk down to murder," where the battlefield is a "burning cemetery" on which "sausages of battle" move about, headed for "the big tearing apart."[14] Characterized by its notably obscene language, Céline's novel—which immediately received a favorable review from Bataille[15]—also deserves mention for a brief and sarcastic reflection that anticipates a classic theme of Bataille's. Céline, who had served in the First World War and been a doctor in Paris until 1932, wrote: "This body of ours, a travesty of agitated and banal molecules, revolts all the time against this atrocious farce of continued existence. They want to disperse out into the universe, our molecules, as rapidly as possible, these dear ones! They suffer from being only 'us,' cuckolds of infinity."[16]

Anxiety at the "loss of one's own I" could have no more cynical and desacralizing formulation. In contrast to literature of this type, "which advocates the ecstatic disappearance of the 'I' into a violent and organic 'we,'"[17] Arendt's general thesis is that the critique of liberal society advanced in the name of disgust for the bourgeois values of utility and security, against which is set the joyous loss of one's own I, has a certain complicity with that principle of the superfluity of human beings that was put into practice in the extermination camps. Obviously there is no question of direct complicity, following the model, which Arendt regards as false, of necessary causal concatenation. But it is a question of highlighting a significant relation between the liberatory exaltation of horror and its extreme practice. Arendt was convinced that the experience of the First World War, far from curing the enthusiasm for violence of the front generation, fueled ideas that exalted the vitalizing function of slaughter and massacre. She was likewise convinced that, in a setting in which "destruction without mitigation, chaos and ruin as such assumed the dignity of supreme values," such ideas end by lending support to an ontological crime whose reach extends well past a simple nihilistic outburst.[18] Her reference to Bataille is inscribed in exactly this argumentative context, which seems to suggest that, for Arendt, there is an alarming continuity between the post-1918 stance promoting the sacrificeability of the self and the theses expounded at the end of the 1940s by Bataille.

Although Arendt mentions Bataille's writings on Sade only in a note, they fit easily into the line of thought she was developing. This is true especially regarding Bataille's insistence on the rupturing of the limits of the I experienced in sexual frenzy and on the "violence inflicted on a human like us" that, extracting the I from the order of finite things, "gives it over to immensity."[19] Bataille's hermeneutic on the horror of the scene in which the I, passing "from a state of autonomy and of being folded in on itself, to a state of opening, of wounding,"[20] gives in to the voluptuousness of its own decomposition, inevitably had to disquiet the author of *The Origins of Totalitarianism*. After all, the Bataille of the essays on Sade was dedicating his intense and original, but also participatory, reading to an extreme theater of violence, centered on a killer shedding the blood of helpless victims. The coincidence postulated between death and eros is unequally distributed between the two parties.

Far from being a matter of chance, as Bataille himself admits, this is an intrinsic limit to sovereign subjectivity, which, albeit erotically attracted by the dissolution of its own nothing, must in the end admit that it is not given to the living being to live "in the moment in which he truly dies" or at any rate to have the genuine "impression of truly dying."[21] Sade's work does not, moreover, belong on the plane of reality but on that of fiction. It still has to do with the fictitious character typical of a certain version of sacrifice: a sacrifice that, for Bataille, can fully manifest its sovereignty only if the sacrificer succumbs and is lost along with his victim.[22]

Into Bataille's complex intellectual biography—obsessed by constant but never linear themes—there flowed highly diverse elements, deriving from the artistic experience of surrealism, from a certain anthropology alert to the dimension of the sacred, from religion, from psychoanalysis, from sociology, and, last but not least, from literature. As Derrida has emphasized, however, along with Nietzsche, it is above all Hegel—read through the celebrated filter of Kojève[23]—who plays the decisive role. From Hegelian thought, Bataille draws, first of all, the distinction between finite and infinite, albeit releasing it from any dialectic movement that would organize it into a system and above all transporting it into the sphere of eros and sexuality. The figure of the finite thus becomes the intolerable limit of a singular life that, in the sovereign man, is attracted precisely by its dissolution into the totality of the infinite, an event that both death and sexual frenzy allow (especially when they are simultaneous), bearing the individual outside himself in the delirium that exceeds his own finiteness. The novelty obviously does not lie in the ancient linkage of Eros and Thanatos but rather, more in homage to Nietzsche than to Freud, in a certain insistence on the virile instincts of destruction, which Bataille tends to reinforce, and justify, through an appeal to the voluptuousness of deindividualization of the orgiastic and violent sort. In this festival of sovereignty, which has "no other aim than the climax of violence, nor other experience than that of *bodies*, eroticized, killed, sacrificed,"[24] there is a certain eager propensity for the theme of the orgy that should not be underestimated. As Jean-Luc Nancy reminds us, "this fascination [with fascism] is not to be taken lightly, no more in Bataille's case than in the case of several others."[25] The perverse interweaving of noteworthy theoretical density and morbid attraction to bloodshed is part of the reason for Bataille's current reputation.

What is certain is that, against the instinct of self-preservation seen as an act wherein the I closes in on itself, it is the death wish that defines the liberty of the sovereign soul. Through death, Bataille states in *L'Érotisme*, the discontinuous beings that we are dissolve, not without voluptuousness and trembling, into the continuity of being, setting themselves free of the condition that attaches them to mortal individuality. In fact, "it is, in its entirety, the elementary being which is at stake [*en jeu*] in the passage from discontinuity to continuity. Only violence can put everything at stake in this way."[26] That such violence—or violation bordering on death and murder—should belong to eroticism is justified for Bataille (rather traditionally and yet crucially) by the fact that the essence of love is "the substitution of a marvelous continuity between two beings for their persistent discontinuity."[27] In this sense, "avid to torture" and faithful to the truth of inebriation that comes from contact with the infinity of the continuous,[28] Sade, at least through the mediation of the helpless victim, did in fact go right to the end.

Disgusting and bloodcurdling (and not by chance), Bataille's conception of violence insists above all on an unleashing of eros with the putative virtue of realizing the unconfessable truth of the finite as self-annihilation in the impersonal law of the flesh. It is the flesh here, rather than the body, that constitutes the vehicle of an ontology that, freely recomposing Hegelian modules, aims at the absolute negation, without residues, of the finite. Individual finiteness—or, better, the singularity of existence—is thus viewed structurally from the vantage point of destruction. Once again, in accord with a philosophical tradition running from Plato to the present, Bataille explains to us that the human being, especially since it is embodied, is *for* death: a death that, from the perspective of the infinite, of which the flesh is the vehicle, becomes the death of anyone, given or received, or, even better, reciprocally exchanged. The undisputed protagonist of this natural voluptuousness of destruction is a violence that works on the suffering body, reawakening the infinite and deindividualized flesh to which it, ontologically, aspires. Horror is thus destruction of human singularity, but it is nevertheless the necessary, as well as sacral, scene on which there operates the frenetic violence of a destroyer who turns out, tellingly, to be immune from any ethical or political responsibility.

It is worth pointing out in this connection that in recent years several refined readings of Bataille, starting with that of Jean-Luc Nancy, have attempted to link his thought to a conception of community in which the very categories of ethics and politics are seen as undergoing a radical reconfiguration. It is Bataille's concept of communication as "mutual destruction" that makes this an interesting perspective.[29] Emphasis falls on a laceration of the self that is an opening vis-à-vis the other, on the self-excess of a singular being who in this way touches "the extreme point of its singularity, the end of its finitude; that is to say the confines upon which compearance with and before the other occurs, without respite."[30] Following Nancy, the fundamental thesis is that, in naming communication the moment at which two beings who are "lacerated, suspended, both leaning over their own nothingness,"[31] put themselves "at stake" [*en jeu*], Bataille was driven to think a subjectivity that is no longer shut up in the arrogance of the self-sufficient individual of modernity but rather open, passively exposed to the other and disposed to encounter it in a reciprocal exposure that has its essential cipher in the sharing out of death. Roberto Esposito calls it "community of death," emphasizing how, as early as the 1930s, the sacred, for Bataille, was "that which puts existence into play, inscribing it within the necessity of a death in common."[32] Conforming to this is a conception of passivity "understood as that passion-suffering that puts existences into communication on the basis of that which continually subtracts them from themselves."[33] Hence, in the last analysis, it is the relation between existences that together gaze into the abyss of their own nothingness that gives rise to community.

Within this theoretical horizon, which has the merit of opposing any nostalgia for communion as well as all the atomized figures of the individual, the recuperation of Bataille is in fact inscribed in the thought of a community of which the relation of every finite being, precisely as finite being, to the other constitutes the essence. This, as Nancy says, is the exact opposite of "the fascist masses, [who] tend to annihilate community in the delirium of an incarnated communion,"[34] as it is of the concentration and extermination camps. As Arendt would probably have pointed out, though, some doubt still clings to Bataille with respect to fascist mass delirium and even more to the scene of extermination. It is telling in fact that the new theorists of community tend to cast a veil of silence over Bataille's committed affinity for orgy, torture, and bodily suffering, as well as his obsessive insistence on eroticism understood in terms of violence and violation. It is precisely these "indecent" aspects that underlie the notable success Bataille has had with a wide area of modern thought about horror.

# 11

###### ▬

# So Mutilated that It Might Be the Body of a Pig

*. . . a picture of a Marine holding an ear or maybe two ears or,*
*as in the case of a guy I knew near Pleiku, a whole necklace*
*made of ears, "love beads" as its owner called them.*

—Michael Herr, *Dispatches*

In her last book, returning to the theme of photography, Susan Sontag chose to reflect on images of horror. Entitled *Regarding the Pain of Others* and published in 2003, the book has a basic message. Sontag maintains that, however much photographs of horror may arouse a morbid pleasure, thus straying into the overcrowded domain of pornography, they have an "ethical value" because they make us aware "that human beings everywhere do terrible things to one another."[1] Virginia Woolf was thinking along similar lines when, defending her antiwar ideas in the celebrated essay *Three Guineas*, she adduced a photograph published in the papers "of what might be a man's body, or a woman's; it is so mutilated that it might, on the other hand, be the body of a pig."[2] Sontag endorses this interpretation of images of horror in a pacifist vein. But she also notes that, in the case of photographs documenting atrocities, the discourse is highly complex and needs to be examined with care.

Such photographs can also serve to foment hatred for the enemy, to trigger vengeance and spur patriotic feeling, swelling the flux of violence. They may also draw the accusation of offending sensibilities and going past the limits of good taste and thus incur censorship. This is especially true, Sontag notes, in contemporary Western societies, which, albeit prepared to contemplate the atrocious suffering of the peoples of the third world in photographs, tend to ban the publication of blood-curdling images when they feature citizens of the first world. The problems arising from the photographic documentation of horror are, in sum, anything but straightforward. After examining them in detail, however, Sontag not only insists on the need to make public all the photographs that record the atrocities inflicted by man on his fellow man but (revising some of her own earlier thinking) goes on to contest the view that their effect is dulled by repetition, leading eventually to saturation. The theme is important, because it involves the role of images in the so-called society of spectacle.

Her final paragraphs take issue with those, like Baudrillard, who insist on the weight of spectacle and the media, in a world of images that has by now supplanted that of reality. Raw reality does exist, especially in photographs of horrors, Sontag stubbornly maintains. To be spectators, by means of images, of the pain of others does not signify that their suffering is not endured materially. The provincial rhetoric of voyeurism—a "French specialty,"[3] according to Sontag—not only fails to cancel out reality; it does not prevent reality from challenging us, making us responsible.

It is in just this context that the Frenchman Bataille earns a mention. Defining him as "one of the great theorists of the erotic," Sontag reminds us that on his desk he kept a photo taken in China in 1910 that featured the torn body of a prisoner undergoing the torture of the "hundred cuts." Sontag describes it thus: "The already armless sacrificial victim of several busy knives, in the terminal stage of being flayed . . . and still alive in the picture, with a look on his upturned face as ecstatic as that of any Italian Renaissance Saint Sebastian."[4]

The reference to Saint Sebastian is not casual. A reproduction of the photograph of the "hundred cuts" actually appears in *The Tears of Eros*, Bataille's last book, in which he undertakes to illustrate the erotic ecstasy of extreme horror with a gallery of images running from archaic cultures to the contemporary era.[5] Through this iconic triumphal parade of the worst torture, the thesis of the coincidence of eroticism and sadism is confirmed yet again in the last book of Bataille, composed when he was ill and close to death. Although Sontag maintains that "it is a view of suffering, of the pain of others, that is rooted in religious thinking, which links pain to sacrifice, sacrifice to exaltation,"[6] Bataille does not dwell here on the Christian martyrs, directing his gaze instead to medieval representations of hell. In his search for "the turbid feeling in which vertiginous horror joins with inebriation,"[7] his enthusiasm is directed especially to raped, flayed, dismembered bodies, to that disfigurement of the human being that ruptures its boundaries and nullifies its singularity. In this sense, the medieval hell is paradigmatic, as is Gilles de Rais, a real person who lived in the fifteenth century and murdered dozens or perhaps hundreds of children and "had their bodies cruelly opened up, and took delight in the sight of their inner organs."[8] Bataille also dedicated a separate study to Gilles de Rais,[9] a personality who seems to deserve an exemplary role just because he discharged his violence on children, the defenseless ones par excellence. In this sense, he incarnates the complete figure of sadism, specifically a sadism for which, notwithstanding his old theories on the death of the sacrificer, Bataille appears to have a fresh appreciation in its unilateral dynamic. That is confirmed by the photograph of Chinese torture which, at the end of the volume, offers the image of a victim helpless and absolutely impotent before his torturers.

Bataille's obsession with the photograph in question is really notable: the first time he saw it, as he confesses, "I was so shaken that I fell into ecstasy."[10] Horror as dismembering gives Bataille great pleasure. He kept the photograph on his desk for decades and never tired of contemplating the suffering of the tortured man, who, tied and suspended, his arms already cut off, is being skinned alive while a "sacrificer" cuts off one of his legs and the crowd follows the stroke of the knife with its gaze. The fact that this is unilateral violence against a helpless person constructs a decisive point for Bataille. Even if the scene appears to deal with a public punishment following a regular sentence, the butchers are not punishing a guilty person here; rather they are dismembering, undoing, disfiguring a human being who, like Medusa, is forced to watch his own destruction. However enormous and intolerable its cruelty, their ontological crime thus goes beyond the bounds of cruelty. It simultaneously presents the extreme side of the vulnerable, here coinciding with the helpless, and the extreme violence that strikes him. In this sense, it is worth repeating, Bataille's tastes bring the profound nucleus of horror fully to light—a light, however, that not only obscures this same nucleus with the pleasures of eros and the myths of a deindividualizing fusion of bodies but above all shuts off the vision of the other side of the vulnerable, the side that yearns for care.

Sontag notes that every image showing the violation of a body is pornographic and that "images of the repulsive can also allure."[11] But not all images of tortured bodies fall into this category for her. Representations of the passion of Christ "and the inexhaustible visual catalogue of the fiendish executions of the Christian martyrs" are representations that aim above all to arouse compassion for those who are suffering or to supply a model of faith and force of spirit.[12] While pointing out the combination in religious iconography of the suffering body and nudity, Sontag's emphasis is not on the pleasures of voyeurism but on the moral implications of such representations. It remains the case, as the author does not fail to note, that here we are dealing with painted or sculpted representations, not photographs. With respect to the suffering undergone by a real body—that same singular body that violence disfigures into the form of a pig, as Virginia Woolf would say—photography makes a quantum leap. Even if he recalls the images of

Saint Sebastian, the Chinese prisoner who, still alive, raises his eyes heavenward is not an artistic creation. He is, as Sontag says, "a photograph, not a painting; a real Marsyas, not a mythic one."[13] This still says nothing about the complex question of the history of the imaginary, but it does say a lot about the difference between representation and reality.

The spellbinding side of horror, relative to "an appetite for sights of degradation and pain and mutilation,"[14] remains in any case an almost obligatory reference, in homage to a certain tendency in contemporary aesthetics, and Sontag does not analyze it further. It seems indeed that the problem does not have to do with the logical effort to reconcile a sexual attraction to horror and the ethical role of the photographs that depict it but rather with the disgust that drives some to avert their gaze altogether.

\* \* \*

On our television screens we rarely see the dismembered bodies of the suicide bombers who blow themselves up in the midst of crowds. In North America and Europe at any rate, these images are censored. But in addition to the photo gallery on the Internet, we have available texts of various kinds that describe them in detail. Repugnance for the work of horror comes, for that matter, not just from looking but also from imagining. And it is a well-known fact, although it is interpreted variously, that among the numerous phenomena of violence present in the world today, that of human bombs arouses particular disgust.

In this connection, Jacqueline Rose poses the question of why, in the case of suicide bombers, the horror is especially linked to the fact that the killer also dies and, more generally, why dying along with one's victims should appear to be a worse act than one in which the attacker does not die. Her answer is that "perhaps . . . the revulsion stems partly from the unbearable intimacy shared in their final moments by the suicide bomber and her or his victims."[15] This would be an intimacy of bodies that explode together and become mingled, a species of "community in death" that, however, renounces the erotic aspects that Bataille would no doubt have attributed to it.

Gayatri Chakravorty Spivak's interpretation of the same phenomenon is, by contrast, decidedly erotic. Here are a few passages from a lecture she gave in June 2002 at a conference at the University of Leeds, which have caused much controversy on the Internet:

Suicide bombing—and the planes of 9/11 were living bombs—is a purposive self-annihilation, a confrontation between oneself and oneself, the extreme end of autoeroticism, killing oneself as other, in the process killing others. It is when one sees oneself as an object capable of destruction in a world of objects, so that the destruction of others is indistinguishable from the destruction of self.

Suicidal resistance is a message inscribed on the body when no other means will get through. It is both execution and mourning, for both self and other. For you die with me for the same cause, no matter which side you are on. Because no matter who you are, there are no designated killees in suicide bombing. No matter what side you are on, because I cannot talk to you, you won't respond to me, with the implication that there is no dishonor in such shared and innocent death.[16]

Although this reading of the suicidal act also evokes the plane of "resistance" in a politically desperate situation, it is principally the erotic communication of bodies united by a violent death that functions as the interpretive horizon here. She does not cite Bataille explicitly, but Chakravorty Spivak is clearly referring to the language of a certain radical psychoanalysis in which, in various ways but in any case by a "French route," Bataille's discourse has left its sediment. It is thus no surprise that, despite the political reference to "resistance," the protagonists of this "innocent" and "shared" death are stripped of their political part—of their cause and identity—in order to communicate with one another as singularities. This, in homage to postmodern theory, is obviously already characterized by an internal work of alterity that permits the suicide to kill herself as another while she is killing others. In this manner, horror here assumes the ambiguous figure of a violent destruction that is, at the same time, an opening of the self as self-annihilation and communication with the other in the act of assassinating him. The myths of the sacred and the sacrificeability of oneself are not very far off. Also too near is a conception of horror that not only exalts its erotic side but insists on gazing on the vulnerable, struck in a situation in which he is circumstantially helpless, uniquely from the side of destruction. In this destruction, dealing as we are with a simultaneous death imposed unilaterally by the suicide bomber, there seems not to be any reciprocity, as a certain conception of communication would, in all rigor, require. In this case, horrorism doesn't seem to take a subtle approach: the category of "community" matches up with "reciprocity" as much as it does with "unilaterality" and, what is more, confuses them.

Bataille, as glossed by Klossowski, affirms that "every 'communication' participates in suicide and crime."[17] From Bataille's perspective, my opening myself to "communion," as well as obviously implicating the other, implies above all that I destroy "the integrity of being, in myself and in the other." The problem, which can be traced back to the model of sacrifice and sadism, is always the same and reveals a structural contradiction. On one hand,

Bataille maintains "that 'communication' cannot take place from one full and intact being to another: it requires beings who have *put at stake* [*mis en jeu*] the being in themselves, placed it at the limit of death, of nothingness." In this way the reciprocity of putting oneself in play constitutes the essence of communication. On the other hand, however, he goes on to reflect on the various scenarios of "communication" in which, ignoring reciprocity, it is the unilateral act of the destroyer that puts the other at stake, forcing him, with violence, to disintegrate. The fact that the destroyer is a suicide who, contrary to Sade and in conformity to sacrifice in its complete form, dies with his victim, obviously doesn't change the unilaterality of the act. "Every 'communication' participates in suicide and crime" is Bataille's thesis. Some interpretations of contemporary horrorism appear to share, and appreciate, it.

# 12

■

# The Warrior's Pleasure

*"By God, that looks like a bloody good show!"*
—W. G. Sebald, *On the Natural History of Destruction*

When Arendt insists on the relation between theories that look for the sublime in the infamous, "elevating cruelty to the highest virtue," and the experience of the front generation, she brings an important theme into focus. The First World War was not just one of the many wars that, from Homer's day to ours, have covered the planet with blood. It inaugurated the model of total war, perfected in the 1939–1945 conflict and characterized by "the placing of civilians on the same level as military personnel, and the propensity to exterminate them without hesitation."[1] The traditional, even heroic conception that defined it as "a duel on a larger scale," a fair battle between uniformed soldiers, was definitively abolished. Soldiers continued to fight, obviously, while terror and horror, as essential forms of the phenomenology of war, beset them more than ever. But the scenario changed radically. It changed for the soldiers themselves, sent to be slaughtered in droves. But, with a decisive acceleration in the Second World War, it changed above all for civilians, who, in the overall victim count, grew in number to become the large majority. Organized destruction, heightened by the technology of modern weapons while still pretending to focus on the classic figure of the warrior, redirected its aim at the defenseless, revealing a distinct horrorist signature, over the course of the twentieth century.

According to Marcello Flores, "it has been calculated that, in round figures, those killed during the twentieth century in acts of mass violence numbered between one hundred and one hundred and fifty million (some have even spoken of a figure of two hundred million)."[2]

The proportion of civilians killed reached 50 percent in the course of the Second World War and exceeded 90 percent during the last decade of the century. As for the first years of the new millennium, it would seem from the sources available that the figure is even higher. Confining ourselves to the twentieth century and civilian victims in Europe, when it comes to horrorism we are compelled to begin with the series of genocides that, reactualizing a long tradition,[3] imparted a new meaning to the phrase "slaughter of the innocents." The view is by now widely shared that "the massacre of millions of men, carried out with complete impunity, could succeed precisely because those men were innocent."[4] The quoted passage refers to the Stalinist Lagers that began to swallow up Soviet citizens in 1937, but the list obviously must commence with the million Armenian citizens of the Ottoman Empire deported to their deaths in the desert, before moving on to the mass extermination that totaled almost six million dead among Jews alone in the Nazi camps. In different geographical settings, and including the victims of "induced famines,"[5] victims numbering in the millions are also reported in the case of the Maoist regime in China and Pol Pot's Cambodia, which achieved the extermination of 20 percent of the population.

Any review of the refined arts of war developed over the course of the century would have to dedicate a separate chapter to the aerial bombardments inaugurated by German forces over Guernica and Coventry. The thesis, shown to be totally unrealistic, was that mass mortality among the inhabitants of populous cities would sap their morale and that of the troops at the front. Churchill thought so, ordering the bombardment of German cities so that "those who have loosed these horrors upon mankind will now in their homes and persons feel the shattering strokes of just retribution."[6] Under the bombs of the Royal Air Force, which used both explosives and incendiaries in such a way that even in shelters the victims died, by being "cooked," one hundred and fifty thousand people died in Dresden alone, and the total for Germany was six hundred thousand; in Tokyo, more than two hundred thousand died. The victims of the great horrorist mushroom inaugurated by the atomic bombs over Hiroshima and Nagasaki in August 1945 exceeded two hundred thousand. Passing to the second half of the century—after the Geneva Convention of 1949 defined the killing of innocent civilians as a war crime—the three million dead in the Vietnam War, the majority of them defenseless victims of napalm bombing, deserve mention. In the realm of civil war, there is the primitive horror of genocide by machete that reached a daily average of forty-nine hundred victims in Rwanda. And in the intestine war in the Balkans, "the Dayton accords signed on 21 November 1995 left a heritage of two hundred and fifty thousand dead, fifty thousand persons tortured, and an equal number of women raped."[7] As for rape, the most notorious episode of the twentieth century remains the Nanking massacre in which, in 1937, Japanese troops unleashed their fury on the civilian population, especially women, old people, and children. During the early years of the present century, the area of greatest suffering has been Iraq, where from 2003 through the first half of 2006 the estimated total number of deaths among the population comes close to six hundred thousand.[8] This list is obviously arbitrary and incomplete.

Nor is it a question of numbers, even if a focus on quantities is inevitable when we are dealing with mass homicide.[9] The numbers serve merely to emphasize how butchery and carnage are now directed—in the bulk of cases, although not exclusively—at the civilian population. In an epoch of "mass death unprecedented in history,"[10] to continue to discuss war in terms of regulated conflict between states, in line with the classical and "symmetrical" model of a clash between men in uniform, is, in this sense, misleading. The kind of war that matured in the twentieth century and looms over the new millennium is not only asymmetric, as were and are all colonial wars, but, like them, consists predominantly of the homicide, unilateral and sometimes planned, of the defenseless. Nor does the rhetorical expedient, typical of military language, of "collateral damage" do any good: on the factual plane, it does not succeed in masking the existence of "the blown-off limbs, the punctured eardrums, the shrapnel wounds, and the psychological horror that are caused by heavy bombardment."[11] Struck one by one, in the singularity of their vulnerable bodies, the helpless ones stand at the center of modern destruction and highlight its drift into horrorism. This places them in a position of perspective on horror that, in speaking of war, no discussion ought any longer ignore.

Often execrated as a tremendous evil and as the maximal expression of human violence, war has been regarded as inevitable for millennia. But the modern age especially has been able to make use of theories that, variously articulated and cutting across different disciplinary levels, have succeeded in endowing this inevitability with a natural foundation. I refer to theories, originating in the early twentieth century and not untouched by the eroticization of horror already discussed, that trace violence back to "aggressiveness, defined as an instinctual drive, [that] is said to play the same functional role in the household of nature as the nutritive and sexual instincts in the life process of the individual and the species."[12] This is Arendt's characterization, in an essay from the 1960s in which she imputes this naturalistic acceptation of violence primarily to the modern social sciences. As the author implies, the term "social sciences" is not to be taken in a narrow sense. It is meant simply as a comprehensive label for the various fields of knowledge that emphasize the pulsional origin of the phenomenon of violence. At the dawn of the modern era, for that matter, Hobbes was already speaking of war as part of human nature, in his celebrated description of the state of nature as a state of war. The modern social sciences, to stay with Arendt's thesis, go a step further, however: they ascribe war, like violence, not just to "an irrepressible instinct of aggression" but also to "a secret death wish of the human species."[13] Thus Freud and psychoanalysis inevitably come to the foreground.

The Freudian idea of a death wish is well known: "a death instinct, the task of which is to lead organic life back into the inanimate state."[14] He describes it as a drive that, albeit originally directed inward in the form of self-destructiveness, also projects outward, "against the external world and other organisms."[15] In other words, and to adopt the technical imprecision of Arendtian terminology, it is a desire for death that is at the same time an instinct of aggression. As is equally well known, Freud developed this theme during the final phase of the writings in which, from 1914 to 1922, he described the functioning of psychic activity. The background is the period during and shortly after the First World War, an epoch in which death and destruction were operative on a vast scale. It should also be noted that, as proof of the plausibility of the intrinsic linkage between the death wish and the impulse of destruction, he resorts to an argument taken from the field of biology; to be precise, he describes the passage from single-cell organisms to multicellular ones in terms of a death wish that, instead of directing its destructive impulse inward toward the single cell, is redirected outward. So when Arendt denounces the naturalistic conception of violence derived from the "modern social sciences," she hits the mark: the incursion into the field of the natural sciences is a salient trait of psychoanalytic theory in its formative phase. Rather than at Freud, though, the denunciation ought to be directed at the immense success of certain Freudian categories in the second half of the twentieth century, especially at the way they have been absorbed and reworked, if not hypostasized, by the various disciplines that have intersected with psychoanalysis, one way or another, over the course of the century. The phenomenon is, to put it mildly, conspicuous. Especially on the plane of media popularization, the century saw the expansion of a horizon of meaning within which the death wish along with the destructive impulses, and not seldom their horrorist side à la Bataille, acquired the status of established, unquestionable, and evident principles. Any reflection on violence in general and war in particular was virtually obliged to take them into account.

At the start of the third millennium, in other words in the era of so-called global war, a prime example of this is a book published in the United States by James Hillman in 2004. It is entitled *A Terrible Love of War* and is based on the Jungian theory of archetypes. But the book stands out not because of the reference to Jung, or to psychoanalysis in general, but because of the nonchalance with which Hillman recuperates and mixes together the main strands of twentieth-century naturalistic thought on violence to corroborate his thesis. He maintains that war "belongs to our souls as an archetypal truth of the cosmos"[16] and that this archetypal truth is, as the title of his second chapter puts it, "normal." He proceeds with an analysis of the theme of a horror that remains human even in its atrocious inhumanity, adding that war is sublime and belongs to the sphere of religion.[17] "If war is sublime, we must acknowledge its liberating transcendence and yield to the holiness of its call."[18] This does not mean, obviously, that Hillman wishes for a perpetual state of war. His aim is rather to get rid of the "pacifist rhetoric" that, in denying the natural—psychic—root of the phenomenon, impedes comprehension of it.

As the reader will easily intuit, while the authors cited (often inappropriately) are highly disparate, it is principally categories deriving from psychoanalysis, the sociology of the sacred, and the anthropology of sacrifice that underpin the articulation of Hillman's discourse. The theoretical density, as well as the internal problematics of these categories, which in his text are forced to undergo drastic simplification, are transformed into banal clichés. In order to justify war as an unrenounceable and vital experience, Hillman often appeals not just to the authority of his authors but to a so-called common opinion that by now constitutes the vulgate, in the form of the stereotypical and the obvious, of those same authors. An example is the facility with which he takes for granted "our fascination with war films, with weapons of mass destruction, with pictures of blasted bodies and bombs bursting in the air."[19] To this Hillman adds, on a confessional note, "the fascination, the delight in recounting the dreadful details of butchery and cruelty. Not sublimation, the sublime."[20] Typical as well in the way it casts a shadow of abnormality—if not pathological stupidity or obtuseness—over those who do not share the fascination with butchery, Hillman's thesis has its own stringent logic. Once violence is rooted in the natural realm of the impulses or, if one prefers, in the archetypical order of the cosmos, the horror of war cannot fail to transmit its fascination both to everyone's visual experience and to the literary practice of some. And, even more logically, it is combatants with firsthand experience in the field who savor the full fascination. The words of the soldiers that Hillman diligently reports in his text for the purpose of documenting his theory prove it. Among them, the words of a cinematographic version of General Patton stand out, when, faced with the devastation of battle and kissing a dying officer, he exclaims, "I love it. God help me, I do love it so. I love it more than my life." Then there is the authentic declaration of a marine who confesses, "The thing I wish I'd seen—I wish I could have seen a grenade go into someone's body and blow it up." No one else, though, rivals the laudable capacity to synthesize of the anonymous American soldier who, in describing a bayonet charge, defines it as "awful, horrible, deadly, yet somehow thrilling, exhilarating."[21]

In the name of a realism grounded in the power of cliché, the entire repertory of war's horror is thus reduced by Hillman to the realm of enjoyment. "The savage fury of the group, all of whose members are out for one another's blood," which the celebrated work of René Girard inscribes in the phenomenology of ritual,[22] becomes the trivial wage of the warrior. For that matter the stereotype of the soldier excited by killing has a long and prestigious history. A certain arousal by violence was already characteristic of Homer's warriors, and the warmongering rhetoric of every age, ennobled by writers and poets, is full of soldiers made happy by death. The events of the twentieth century, and even more those occurring right now, might suggest to the singers and scholars of massacre that they change register. Today it is particularly senseless that the meaning of war and its horror—as well, obviously, as its terror—should still be entrusted to the perspective of the warrior. If it is true, as the historian Giovanni De Luna laments, that "wars, with the violence and cruelty they unleash, appear to have a common ground (killing and getting killed), always the same and impervious to chronology,"[23] it is also true that only warriors, after all, fit this paradigm. The civilian victims, of whom the numbers of dead have soared from the Second World War on, do not share the desire to kill, much less the desire to get killed. Nor does the pleasure of butchery, on which Hillman insists, appear to constitute a possible common ground in this case. You would have to ask the victims of the bombing, cooked by incendiary bombs in the shelters of Dresden, or those whose skin was peeled off by phosphorous bombs in the Vietnamese villages, where the pleasure and excitement was for them. And you would have to put the same question to the children blown up in many parts of the world by antipersonnel mines or to the engaged couple who, falling like marionettes from the Twin Towers in flames, took final flight in New York on the morning of September 11.

As experts in political and military matters would point out, however, this last case concerns terrorism, not war, which, speaking of today's violence and the horrorist paradigm, constitutes a notoriously difficult problem, one worthy of the closest attention.

# 13

<br>

## Worldwide Aggressiveness

*The old saying "One person's terrorist is another person's freedom*
*fighter" has some truth to it. The designation of terrorism is a*
*subjective judgment about the legitimacy of certain violent acts*
*as much as it is a descriptive statement about them.*
—Mark Juergensmeyer, *Terror in the Mind of God*

illman's book, published in 2004, is exemplary in many respects, one of which is this interesting particular. Although it does include a few references to the events of September 11, 2001, it does not address the problem of distinguishing between war and terrorism. As Arendt would put it, the naturalistic basis of the modern social sciences does not concern itself with isolating the criteria that ultimately define the various forms of violence. Observed from the point of view of a carnage that is enjoyment and excitation, one is as good as another. As long as the horror is sublime, the historical question of who gets it started is just an unimportant detail.

The sciences of politics—understood here in a broad sense—follow the opposite reasoning. Although they are often disposed to define violence in terms of an energy (very natural, alas!) that revitalizes the realm of politics through wars and revolutions, they specialize in distinguishing its various forms. In the modern epoch, this distinction generally emphasizes the difference between regular and irregular violence, tendentially based on the opposition legal/illegal in the juridical meaning of international and constitutional law. Tied to historical contingency and the parabola of the sovereign state, the discourse about this, as well as being a crucial object of debate, is, to put it mildly, complex. But in its elementary grammar, still invoked today when one wishes to distinguish between war and terrorism, it actually refers to a fairly simple schema. Violence connected to the classic model of war between states is seen as regular, indeed legitimate and legal. Violence perpetrated by nonstate actors, on the other hand, is seen as irregular and hence criminal. With its propensity—typical of modern political thought—to ground itself in juridical categories, the argumentation goes on to distinguish among the modes and objectives of war, listing its principles, customs, and rules in detail. Foremost among them is the distinction between military personnel and civilians or, if one prefers, between combatants and noncombatants. From one perspective, this distinction is apparently obvious and traditional, but from another, and perhaps precisely because of a tradition that no longer holds, it is a principle that the events of the twentieth century have laden with telling ambiguity. It is not difficult to point to the forcing of perspective in a theory that insists on formulating the regularity of war in terms of the regularity of the combatants in an age when the victims of violence, regular wars included, are civilians by a wide majority. It would seem that, even for modern political science, the warrior's point of view is hard to let go of. Albeit analyzed in juridical terms rather than in terms of enjoyment and excitation, the scene of violence is still observed from the soldier's viewpoint rather than through the eyes of the defenseless victims. Not that the victims, in their quality as noncombatants and often labeled as collateral damage, are entirely outside the frame in which the regularity or irregularity of violence is adjudicated. It is well known that the Geneva Convention of 1949, together with all the international law it inspired, inscribes the killing of innocent civilians among war crimes. Yet within this frame the fighter still remains the predominant figure. Through a strange persistence in the contemporary imaginary of the "baroque idea that conceives of war as theater," "as a series of battles that take place on a battlefield where the outcome of it is decided,"[1] the figure of the warrior remains at the center of the inquiry and substantiates its criterion.

Made famous by the aphorism that defines war as a continuation of politics by other means, the Prussian general Clausewitz, who distinguished himself on the Napoleonic battlefield, is among the most lucid analysts of the phenomenon of war.[2] His great merit, according to Carl Schmitt, is to have perfected the model of regular war between states, although he did go so far, without drawing out all the implications of his "astonishingly telling remarks,"[3] as to insert the anomalous figure of the modern irregular combatant, or what Schmitt calls the partisan, into his theory of war. The quotation is from a text of Schmitt published in Berlin at the beginning of the 1960s entitled *Theory of the Partisan*. In the context of his argument, "to be a partisan is precisely to avoid carrying weapons openly, the partisan being the one who fights from ambushes, who wears the enemy uniform and whatever insignia serves his turn, as well as civilian clothing, as decoys."[4] In other words, it indicates the irregular combatant as opposed to the soldier in uniform who is the classic protagonist of conflict conducted "between states by regular armies of states, between standard-bearers of a *jus belli* who respect each other at war as enemies."[5] It is well known that the notion of the enemy, as a special category of the political, is of central concern to Schmitt.[6] His thesis in the book in question is that the figure of the irregular combatant compels a rethinking of this category, in other words, that the partisan, as Clausewitz had intuited, changes the interstate model of war and hence of politics. Thus in the 1960s, before globalization was spoken of, much less global terror, Schmitt was already positing the need to "search for a new political control of hostilities, in a now post-state age."[7] What he thematizes—"awareness of the radical collapse of the traditional political form,"[8] in other words, of the decline of the state—is not just the distinction between regular and irregular violence based on the status of the combatant but above all the mode in which, in this new context, the question of the enemy is posed. He highlights the shift from a situation that assumes the reciprocal recognition of the combatants in uniform as enemies to one that allows for attack by combatants without uniforms, invisible because they wear no badges of identification, since "secrecy and darkness are [their] strongest weapons."[9] To label them enemies on the basis of the old model of regular warfare becomes improper. To label them criminals is part of the problem, more a symptom of it than a solution to it, which Schmitt, with great lucidity, registers punctually.

It should be noted that, as Carlo Galli points out in *Theory of the Partisan*, "Schmitt does not examine the figure of the terrorist, which would have provided him with a perfect example."[10] As we make our way through the linguistic and conceptual confusion that characterizes today's debate on the "war on terror," Schmitt's text nevertheless proves extremely useful, especially when, utilizing a range of examples from the Spanish *guerrilleros* of the Napoleonic era to the revolutionaries of Maoist China, Schmitt draws a fundamental distinction between two types of partisan: those who have a real enemy and those who have an absolute enemy. The enemy, the central category of the classic model of war between states, is here examined from the perspective of the irregular combatant. A real enemy, according to Schmitt, occurs in the case of a partisan tied to his own land and able to move easily on it, a "tellurian" partisan who is fighting against an invading or occupying army or against government forces against which he feels enmity. Albeit irregular, he is in substance a defender of his native soil: a resistance fighter or, as we could also call him, an insurgent. An absolute enemy, on the other hand, occurs in the case of a partisan who, cutting loose from the "tellurian" dimension, wages a struggle that aims at world revolution because he identifies his enemy as a class or as the characteristics of any kind of identity (including the Western lifestyle, to give an up-to-date example). Characterized by a worldwide aggressiveness,[11] he is structurally inclined to criminalize his enemy and make every effort to annihilate him. It is worth noting, as Schmitt suggests, that in both cases the history of the West furnishes abundant cultural legitimation to the figures delineated here. Albeit irregular when measured against the criterion of military and state legality in the classic sense, both the insurgent and the international revolutionary can count on an authoritative tradition that declares legitimate, sometimes even ex post facto, their resort to violence. The problem is obviously highly complex, but, demonstrating the utility of the reflections that Schmitt develops in this text, it succeeds at any rate in illuminating the reasons why, in today's debate on terrorism claiming a basis in Islam and more specifically on the bloody explosions in Baghdad and Jerusalem, the label "insurgents" is a crucial topic of discussion. An example is the choice of the BBC—following an editorial debate focused on just this question in 2003—to call those who were fighting against the British and American occupying troops "insurgents" and to use the same term generally for many of the armed opponents of the Iraqi government.[12] Beneath the choice of labels, today particularly urgent and insidious, there is always a problem of concepts.[13] Schmitt notes that, "as a European observer of the old tradition, one has to avoid falling back precisely in this context on conventional, classical concepts of war and peace which, when they speak of war and peace, assume the contained European war of the nineteenth century, with its implication of merely relative and containable enmity."[14]

As Clausewitz had intuited, already with Napoleon, who, according to Marx and Engels, "*perfected* the *Terror* by *substituting permanent war* for *permanent revolution*,"[15] the old tradition was showing signs of strain. But on the historical plane, the decisive turn comes in the twentieth century, when the concept of absolute enemy enters definitively into the lexicon of intraspecies violence. Introduced by the partisan who has abandoned the tellurian dimension, it has to do with a new type of war in which the global space of combat is characterized by "pure means of destruction," in other words, "weapons of absolute annihilation [that] require an absolute enemy lest they should be absolutely inhuman."[16] If the concept of enemy were to lack this qualification of "absolute" that makes it possible to dehumanize him and see him as a morally abject criminal, those who annihilate him "are themselves criminal and inhuman."[17] Insisting on the theme, Schmitt even goes so far as to hypothesize that, in future, "enmity will be so terrifying that one perhaps mustn't even speak any longer of the enemy or of enmity." Becoming totally abstract, destruction will need only to appeal to "another, ostensibly objective attainment of highest values, for which no price is too high to pay."[18] An interesting hypothesis, if not prophetic, to put it mildly.

It is worth noting, in this connection, that the reference, unspoken here but inevitable, to the reality of the Nazi regime—of which Schmitt was at the outset a supporter—throws a fairly sinister, and historically all too well informed, light on the lucidity of this prophecy. After all, for the Nazis the absolute enemy, or as Arendt would say, the "objective enemy,"[19] was the Jew. It is no secret that Schmitt's biography makes appreciating his speculative acumen uncomfortable. Yet his entire corpus not only stands among the major works of political thought of the twentieth century, it constitutes "one of the most extraordinary anticipations of the themes of the global epoch."[20] The usefulness of the small volume *Theory of the Partisan* amply confirms this, for it makes it possible, on one hand, to highlight with a certain precision the theoretical backdrop and the historical hinterland of the current debate on war and terrorism and, on the other, to capture its structural ambiguities. Among these, apart from the problem of the regularity of taking military action against antagonist subjects without state or territorial identity, there stands out the ambiguity flowing from the privileging of the perspective of the warrior, shared by Schmitt himself, which continues to pay its debt to the old and obsolete model of war between states.

In the epoch of the "war on terror," when we are being forced to acknowledge that the distinction between war and terrorism is a crucial problem and likewise to recognize the novelty of the context, both scholars of political and military affairs and the media who simplify their opinions still in fact tend to refer to the classic model of interstate war. Within a theoretical framework created to justify war—and even the highly anomalous concepts of "preventive war" and "humanitarian war"—terrorism is, in substance, accused of differing from it as regards both subjects and methods, of being a criminal form of violence, given that both its actors and its acts are incompatible with the conventional system of destruction. Even if this criterion—which we might call the criterion of the warrior—is often flanked by a principle that, in contrast, takes the status of the victims into account, distinguishing civilian and military ones, the general framework doesn't shift away from the classic model. To put it differently, the argumentation never goes so far as to embrace exclusively, or at any rate radically, the criterion of the defenseless. Instead it tends to repeat, in line with the tradition, that the regular combatant directs his fire against other combatants or the enemy's strategic sites, hitting civilians only by mistake. The terrorist not only does not follow this rule, he most often does aim to kill civilians. This renders him doubly criminal and makes his violence distinct from that of regular troops who have a legitimate government and a state behind them. But when the theory is applied on the plane of events, ambiguities soon emerge.

An example is a thesis to which Charles Townshend alludes in a recent study of terrorism, the brevity of which is accompanied by a rare intellectual honesty.[21] Published in 2002, the book is informed by the specific questions raised by the events of September 11 and after, among which the distinction between war and terrorism appears decisive. "The issue of definition, of distinguishing terrorism from criminal violence or military action,"[22] is the main theme of the current debate, Townshend asserts. Adducing the customary authority of Clausewitz and well aware that he is dealing with a problem rather than a solution, he notes that war is battle, "the collision of two living forces,"[23] whereas terrorism avoids frontal battle, attacking its targets "in a way that inhibits (or better prohibits) self-defence." In synthesis: "the essence of terrorism is the use of violence by the armed against the unarmed," given that, albeit not necessarily innocent in an objective sense, "targets . . . must be in practical terms defenseless ('soft')."[24] The criteria of the warrior and that of the defenseless are thus mingled. On the one hand, emphasis is placed on the regularity of war on the basis of the usual principle that defines it as a clash, fair and equal, so to speak, between armies, a duel on a large scale in which the violence is reciprocal. On the other hand, the criterion that differentiates it from terrorism is identified in victims who · are defenseless and so are struck by unilateral violence. It suffices, though, to cite Hiroshima and Nagasaki—recently listed by Michael Walzer among cases of "war terrorism"[25]—as well as the carpet bombing of cities during the Second World War and subsequent wars, to reveal how weak, above all from the viewpoint of the populations attacked (and certainly limited in self-defense), the overall framework of the argumentation is. On top of that, and with due acknowledgement of the problems of translation, the so-called Islamic terrorists declare themselves soldiers in a just or holy war, and their lexicon, although drenched in religious language that loads it with a particular meaning, is rich in terms that evoke the ardor of battle. To cite Schmitt once again, even the irregular combatant "declares the enemy a criminal and all concepts of law, statute, and honor an ideological fraud."[26] From the point of view of the warrior, the distinction between war and terrorism does indeed lead to ambiguous results. When the warrior's point of view is mixed with that of the defenseless, on the basis of the conviction that they are congruent, the ambiguity immediately becomes contradiction.

Worthy of note, in this sense, is the explanation furnished by the Court of Assizes of Milan for the sentence it delivered on 9 May 2005, concerning "international terrorism." Stating that judges cannot base themselves on "a vague and generic sociological notion of terrorism that claims to derive from an ungraspable common sense" and referring to the case of Iraq, the president of the court specifies that only after the installation of the government of Allawi, the interim prime minister, were the attacks on soldiers of the coalition forces definable as terrorist acts.[27] Before that date, they were regular acts of war against an occupying enemy (in other words, against what Schmitt calls a real enemy; the concord between him and the Milanese judges in qualifying the terrorists as insurgents is significant). The court's sentence in fact excludes any violent action against military forces in a situation of war, independently of its subjects and the mode in which it is carried out, from being called terrorism. As the sentence emphasizes, though, this only holds good in cases in which soldiers are the target. Even in war settings, violent conduct "perpetrated against civilians or persons who are not taking part in the hostilities that are going on" loses its legitimacy and falls squarely into the category of terrorism. The text specifies that such violent conduct is understood to include (significantly, putting them in parentheses): "bombings in schools, car bombs, the capture and killing of hostages." A new series of ambiguities thus arrives once more to upset the logical framework of the argumentation. On one hand, a typical unconventional weapon like a car bomb (and, by obvious extension, suicide bombing) ends up appearing to be regular as long as its victims are occupying soldiers and not civilians. In this case, we would supposedly have not terrorists but insurgents. On the other hand, the equation between terrorism and civilian victims ends by consigning the distinction between war and terrorism to the rhetorical operation that renames civilian victims as collateral damage. As Collins and Glover note, "the need for such language derives from the simple fact that the violence itself is abhorrent," and its aim is to "avert our mental gaze from the physical effects of violence."[28] Given the logic set out here, on what basis does a missile fired by the occupying army at a crowded restaurant in a densely populated quarter of Baghdad not amount to terrorism? Like the "vague and generic sociological notion of terrorism" that the president of the Milanese court rightly rejected, the theory that assumes the regularity of war to distinguish it from terrorism also leads to equivocal and contradictory results. The defenseless person is correctly designated as the illegitimate victim par excellence, but there remains a significant reluctance to take him or her as the exclusive criterion for separating illegitimate from legitimate violence. For that matter, it is not the job of judges to resolve problems of this type, "strengthening the state against terrorism." The task of questioning the conceptual apparatus of modernity about war and violence falls rather to the work of theory, which must make the effort, at last, to break free of the criterion of the warrior, all the more so when "the intermediate link in the modern international order represented by the nation-state has ruptured."[29]

What is certain is that the problem of distinguishing war from terrorism—even understood in terms of the procedures for naming that characterize the current debate—would gain much clarity if the criterion of the defenseless were not contaminated with that of the warrior. One might begin by emphasizing that, although war also kills the defenseless—in fact it now kills them in very high proportions—modern terrorism tends to slaughter them exclusively. It makes a precise strategic choice, as is often noted, in which the killing of some aims to produce a terrorizing effect on everyone. It is precisely this effect that has earned terrorism its very name. It is worth pointing out that, in the case of modern violence summed up under the rubric of Islamist terrorism, we have to force the perspective somewhat to see this effect as part of the physics of terror. Only those who find themselves in physical proximity to the bombing tremble and flee. For the others, the everyone at whom the terrorizing effect is strategically aimed, trembling and flight are replaced by imagining themselves among the actual victims and knowing that it could happen to them. Phantasmic and ungraspable, distant and yet near—the televised images on which the authors of terrorist attacks are counting see to that—terror is there, and it is, classically, fear of violent death. In its instinctual movement, the physics of terror is blocked, however, dispersing into the unforeseeable contingency of future time and everywhere. Terror today is "first of all the terror of the next attack."[30]

Disengaged from the intensive continuity of war, the time of violence thus dilates and finishes by coinciding, through unfathomable intermittence, with the banal dimensions of daily life: a sort of homicidal version of so-called glocal. The object of looming destruction that menaces him everywhere and anyhow, the defenseless person becomes the figure of a vulnerability the more perfect in that it is chance that makes him into an exemplary victim. That this exemplarity is involuntary forms part of the so-called strategic framework; indeed, in the era of globalization, it ends by acquiring a sinister, universal valence. Though not for all, for a large proportion of the inhabitants of the globe today, every moment, with greater or less probability according to geography, is now the possible and arbitrary hour of their chance assassination. Obviously, random death has to multiply and renew itself, keep its potential victims on edge and massacre a few, in order for its effects not to be canceled by adaptation to the perpetual menace of terror, of which human beings have shown they are capable. But is this really terror?

It may be defined more prudently, in Schmittian terms, as a form of violence, stripped of visible markers and characterized by a worldwide aggressiveness that identifies the "infidel" as the absolute enemy and merges him with the defenseless. Notwithstanding Schmitt and others, the viewpoint of the defenseless must not only be adopted here, it must be adopted exclusively; that is what really matters. If seen on the basis of the warrior criterion, the same scene, while remaining atrocious, ends by losing its peculiarity and becoming ambiguous once more. On one hand, it represents a self-described combatant who, making war on "infidels" in the name of "true Islam," identifies the absolute enemy with a category so wide that it comprises both soldiers and civilians and is, above all, structurally ill suited to supplying any reason to differentiate between them. On the other hand, it represents a use of terror that, with respect to the objective of annihilating the infidels, unarmed or in uniform, can only appear to be strategic and thus raise the classic question of means and ends typical of traditional political and military doctrine.

The attitude of separating strategy and goals, including in terms of juridical or moral evaluation, is well known to belong to the mentality of the warrior and the state actor that legitimates him. The history of modern warfare, to restrict our focus to that, is full of irregular strategies, genuine massacres of defenseless people, and slaughters on a large scale justified in the name of higher, more just ends. There is no question here of bringing in the theme, which has become notoriously topical, of so-called just war,[31] but of registering that "the policy of attacking the civilian population in order to induce an enemy to surrender, or to damage his morale, seems to have been widely accepted in the civilized world, and seems to be accepted still," on the basis of "a moral conviction that the deliberate killing of non-combatants— women, children, and old people—is permissible if enough can be gained by it."[32] Nor would it be worthwhile, in this setting, to mention once more the atomic bombs at Hiroshima and Nagasaki, were it not that their tragic example attests how problematic it is, from the warrior point of view, to apply the name "terrorism" to a strategy in the same context in which one distinguishes terrorism from war in order to criminalize it. If the name is to be maintained, then it falls to whomever finds themselves in the involuntary position of defenseless victim to authorize that. From their point of view, the strategy that strikes them is, as violence unilaterally undergone, the entire substance. Neither means nor end, it consists in the unappealable actuality of mere destruction.

It befalls the defenseless person today to get killed because she happens to pass through certain crowded places, ones chosen by her killers not so much because of the high number of victims to be "obtained" and the consequent media impact, as because anyone could find herself there at that time. It is the defenseless person without qualities, interchangeable and random, who takes the center of the contemporary stage on which the specialists in violence against the defenseless perform. In this sense, to emphasize that "terrorism is the culminating moment of that lack of distinction between civilians and military personnel that has progressively characterized the twentieth century"[33] or that "the division between civilian and military space" is erased by it is still too little.[34] Compared to the violence against civilians shamefully perpetrated by all modern wars for cynical instrumental reasons or even as crude reprisal, the form that is spreading today accomplishes a quantum leap. And not just because today's specialists deliberately aim at the slaughter of innocents but because in this massacre there are not even innocents anymore, given that, whoever they are, each one is as good as the next in the abstract role of example. Although called infidel or miscreant, the absolute enemy loses all quality and assumes the role of anyone at all, with respect to whom the eventual faith of every singular victim—who sometimes, and certainly in modern Iraq, believes in the same god as his murderers—is just an accident. Indeed, it is the very singularity of the victims that is accidental, in observance of the well-known principle of the "superfluity of men" that is now being put into practice by unforeseeable and ubiquitous violence, measured against which any concept of war evaporates. As Arjun Appadurai notes, we are dealing with a paradoxical "quotidian war, war as an everyday possibility, waged precisely to destabilize the idea that there is an 'everyday' for anyone outside the space and time of war."[35] An everyday occurrence, no longer circumscribed in space and time—all the more global in that they are potential and undetermined—it becomes, in other words, an organized violence that nullifies the familiar aspects of its traditional forms. That it resorts to the use of terror is past doubt. But this is a terror that, as Arendt would say, has lost its goals and thus cannot be defined as strategic. It could be called global, rather than total, terror, but the phenomena in which it materializes tend rather toward the realm of horrorism.

The reference to Arendt—but it could have been to Levi, Rousset, or Margarete Buber-Neumann—is not casual here. As a scene of extreme horrorism, governed by a system that does not merely strike the defenseless being but actually manufactures his perverted figure, the Nazi Lager remains a *unicum*. Contemporary horrorism, in the concrete form of so-called global terrorism, especially Al-Qaeda and jihadism, has different traits. The first is a technique of annihilation that focuses on the instant rather than on the process. The defenseless being is not fabricated with methodical persistence but only killed or wounded or mutilated. But not before the circumstance that makes her helpless is dilated into the indeterminacy of a space and a time corresponding to the everyday dimension of the everywhere. Such that, rather than of circumstance we ought properly to speak of an ongoing condition, or, if you like, of a mode of being, that adheres to a great many inhabitants of the planet, albeit with peaks of intensity in hot zones, that makes vulnerability coincide with defenselessness. Exposed unilaterally to *vulnus*, the defenseless are the targets of a violent death that surpasses the event, atrocious in itself, of death, because it has degraded each of them beforehand from singular being to random being.

The English language designates the victims of violent death as casualties. It is a curious expression, inasmuch as "casual" literally means "by chance" or "at random," so a casualty would literally be a randomness. The term is applied in various contexts: hurricanes, floods, buildings that collapse, wars, bombings, and others. As its usage in connection with natural disasters attests, it tends to suggest that we are not dealing with a violence for the purpose of killlling a precise individual but with a violence without specific objectives, whose victims turn out to be, precisely, casual. In a hurricane, some die and some survive, randomly, by good or bad luck, not on account of their singular identities, much less on account of their responsibilities or guilt. Soldiers who are killed in war are also victims of chance, but they have already taken that into account, so to speak. For the civilian victims of war, this prior reckoning is less obvious, and the chance occurrence is thus more tragic. But it is today's horrorism above all that makes the term "casualties" correspond to the reality of helpless victims, assuming a particularly pregnant and etymologically exact sense. More than their death, casualness is what really gives their status as victims substance. Struck just because they are casual, their only value lies in this randomness, which makes them interchangeable and exemplary.

In this sense, albeit dripping with horror (indeed being its most apt theater), war can still count on a certain distinction from pure horrorism. Its casual victims, all the helpless ones it massacres, are difficult to fit into an explicit framework in which their casualty rises to exemplary status. The ontological offense to singularity is there, and it is conspicuous. But it is not yet undergirded by the theoretical coherence that inspires today's "masters of horror."[36] At the level of the butchery, the distinction is much less easy, however, since the balance tips strongly toward war and its propensity to technologize massacre. Precisely because of the technological stamp—from intelligent bombs to weapons of mass destruction—there is, however, a certain crucial difference. More than to advanced technology, the masters of horror tend to entrust the task of dismembering bodies directly to bodies. As the scene of suicide bombing attests, the butchery is substantially an operation of bodies that blow themselves up so as to undo other bodies. Peculiar on account of its stamp of repugnance, this signals a difference not only between the modes of contemporary horrorism and those of war but also between horrorism and terrorism as generally understood. The various historical phenomena grouped under the name terrorism, although they specialize in the massacre of the defenseless, actually do not present any scenario in which the peculiar weapon is the body of a suicide. The latter remains a specialty of the horrorism of our own times. The fact that the history of terrorism, albeit complex and articulated, can acknowledge this specialty as its own ultimate and most recent chapter creates not a little perplexity. Very new, at any rate, is this "perverse mix of sacrificial fideism and calculating-instrumental rationality, which makes the bodies of the 'actors' an organic component of the technological device of destruction."[37]

# 14

###### ▬

# For a History of Terror

*The designation "terrorism" represents an intellectual simplification
that is satisfied with spreading a blanket of disapproval
over things whose logics we cannot easily discern.*
—Gilles Kepel, introduction to *Al-Qaida dans le texte*

As Townshend notes, the term "terrorism" made its first appearance in the 1798 edition of the *Dictionnaire de l'Académie Française*, where it is defined as "système, régime de la terreur."[1] Both the neologism and its definition are influenced by the lexicon of the French Revolution, more specifically by the *Terreur* proclaimed by the Committee of Public Safety in 1793 against the enemies of liberty who were threatening the new republic both externally and internally. But during the two tremendous years that witnessed "the political use of serial death" beneath the blade of the guillotine, the revolutionary patriots directed their terror primarily at the internal enemy, in other words, at citizens of France: unarmed civilians, totaling fourteen thousand victims, of whom "72 per cent came from the same classes that had supported the Revolution."[2] The external threat, on the other hand, continued to be met with the traditional methods of war; in that violent maelstrom, terror persisted as an everyday fact, certainly not as a political category worthy of being distinguished with a capital letter.

Although it was a rhetorical device of revolutionary writing, the importance of that capital letter should not be undervalued. With a certain welcome succinctness, it illuminates the distinction between political Terror and the terror of battle, following a system of correspondences of sorts, in which the place of Terror is the internal sphere of the state and that of terror is the external realm of war. In this system, the terror of battle represents nothing new, being indeed one of its most traditional ingredients. What is new is the state and the Terror that emerges with violence onto the most celebrated of the historical scenes that witness its origin. Born with the state and within the state, terrorism—as one of the categories of its modern classification would have it—emerges into history in the originary form of state terrorism. In this classification, the events in France also mark the onset of so-called revolutionary terrorism, another crucial paradigm for modern history revived principally by the Russian Revolution, in which terror is "an institutional device, consciously employed to accelerate the momentum of the revolution."[3] Given that the Russian case leads precisely to a form of state terrorism, the distinction, at least at this stage of the argument, has little relevance.

Not surprisingly, the lexical contribution of revolutionary France to the history of terrorism finds a significant resonance in the political theory elaborated more than a century earlier by a philosopher prized by Schmitt: Thomas Hobbes, the most lucid and best known of the founding fathers of the modern state as sovereign territorial state. Equally well known is the theoretical construct or, if you prefer, the narrative with which he describes and justifies the artificial genesis of the state or, as he calls it, the "commonwealth." This construct begins with a war, the war of all against all that characterizes the state of nature. It is, says Hobbes, the inevitable consequence of a natural inclination of every man, understood as an atomized individual driven by "a perpetuall and restlesse desire of Power after power, that ceaseth onely in Death."[4] A population of lone wolves prepared to slay one another at any moment, Hobbesian mankind is nonetheless troubled by an internal contradiction: the perpetual desire for power, which makes every competitor merely an obstacle to be eliminated, exposes each one to the perpetual menace of a violent death that puts an end to all his power. In short: every man is inclined to kill others and fears being killed. Thus characterized by the reciprocal will to destroy, the state of nature is presented as a situation belonging to the order of fear. The commonwealth originates as a way of escaping this unbearable and counterproductive situation. It is precisely the fear of imminent death, that is, the desire to keep oneself alive in a situation of peace and security, that drives men to conclude a pact by which they "conferre all their power and strength upon one Man, or upon one Assembly of men, that may reduce all their Wills, by plurality of voices, unto one Will."[5] Unique and hence absolute, like the power that incarnates it, this will coincides with sovereignty, in other words, with the soul of the commonwealth, as being the modern form of politics.

The logic governing the genesis of the commonwealth, however, is presented not just as a transfer of reciprocal natural violence to an artificial center—the sovereign—who holds the monopoly on it but also as a transformation of fear into terror. Hobbes's lexicon is, in this respect, very exact.

If the fear that men provoke in one another prevails in the state of nature, in the commonwealth that makes them citizens there reigns a sovereign power, unique and irresistible, that strikes them with terror.

Without the sword, Hobbes declares, pacts are only words, incapable of guaranteeing any security. Since security is precisely the reason men decide to leave behind the state of nature and transfer all power to the sovereign, the latter must be the only one to wield the sword. In the words of *Leviathan*, "without the terrour of some Power, to cause them to be observed,"[6] the laws in which the will of the sovereign is expressed would have no efficacy, meaning that the requirement of security, as quintessence of the modern state and its legitimation, would have no foundation. It is no accident that the biblical monster who supplies Hobbes with the title of his greatest work has passed into the history of political doctrines as a synonym of terrifying power. Constructed to be irresistible, sovereign power in its Hobbesian version manifests itself through terror. This, it is worth emphasizing once again, is a terror essentially internal to the commonwealth and explicitly aimed at guaranteeing the social order and above all security. The other side of the sovereign's sword, directed toward the external ambit of war against other commonwealths, does not entail a specific use of terror. Obviously this does not mean that in modernity—and Hobbes is well aware of this—terror ceases to present itself as a normal and inevitable aspect of war. But it does mean that when modernity commences, with the Englishman's theory, to reflect in a specific manner on terror, it includes it among the political categories that structure and stabilize the commonwealth. Thus, well before the French Revolution, we have a framework that heralds the appurtenance of terror to the realm of the state (the internal sword), emphasizing at the same time that the waging of war (the external sword) falls exclusively to the state as well. Emblematically, both swords are "regular." In this sense as well, the affinity between the doctrine of Hobbes and later events in France is notable.

Notable for certain is the fact that, for both the English philosopher and Robespierre, terror is not just legitimate but necessary, is indeed a category—respectively foundational and generative—of the state. It took the entire complex sequence that saw the political model of early modernity evolve into its democratic and liberal form (regarded today as the very paradigm of the West) for the state to free itself of its direct relationship to terror and for state terrorism to appear finally as the negation of its essence. Thus, the evident hommage to *Leviathan* notwithstanding, Max Weber's well-known definition, from the second decade of the twentieth century, of the state as the sole legitimate user of violence should not be understood as a simple updating of the Hobbesian doctrine.[7] In the second phase of modernity, which sees the birth and growth of the liberal democracies, quick to justify themselves as the sole alternative to the terror that supposedly characterizes despotic regimes,[8] a significant change comes about in the lexical fabric: although violence, as Weber posits, retains its place in the essential vocabulary of the state, terror has been expelled. No longer appealing to the liberal-democratic state, terror has turned into the perverse mark of regimes that are neither liberal nor democratic, or else it has relocated to a different realm altogether: it now coincides with the violence, labeled irregular—as well as inadmissible and hence criminal from the point of view of the holder of the legitimate monopoly of it—of those who attack the state. And the word for these is "terrorists," exponents of a use of terror defined as totally illicit, morally execrable, and politically incorrect.

While terrorism, on the lexical plane at least, has a precise date of birth, the historical forms in which it has been articulated, from the Terror of the French Revolution to our day, form a heterogeneous and discontinuous pattern that impedes a straightforward definition or at any rate a definition not open to well-founded objections.[9] "Strangely, actual definitions of terrorism are nowhere to be found,"[10] or else, what amounts to the same thing, there are too many of them. The minimal definition, which denotes it as the use of violence for purposes of intimidation, is virtually tautological. Other, more technically precise definitions apply in some cases and not in others. An example is the definition proposed by Giovanni Sartori, for whom the word "terrorism" indicates "the intent to terrorize to the maximum degree, by whatever means and with no target ruled out, the largest possible number of persons." As Sartori makes clear, this definition holds good primarily for "the global and faith-based terrorism of our times."[11]

It is not surprising, then, that "the student of terrorism is confronted with hundreds of definitions in the literature" and that studies focused on this topic, of which there are inevitably many today, tend to devote themselves to a typological, historically documented analysis, applying themselves to a classification of terrorist phenomena rather than to the difficult task of comprising them under a general definition.[12] Albeit anomalous, the pairing of two contraries, state terrorism and terrorism against the state, can still function as a minimal grid, helping to simplify a discourse that does not aim here to be either detailed or exhaustive.

I begin with state terrorism. The first thing to note is that many academic analyses display a certain reluctance to adopt this denomination, preferring to speak of "state terror" or "terrorist regime." Given that the word "terrorism" "conveys a condemnation rather than describes a phenomenology," there is evidently a strong motivation to preclude the possibility "that in general the state as such could be defined as terrorist."[13] But to maintain in principle that "no behavior that bears the chrism of state sovereignty can be considered terroristic" is factious:[14] state terrorism remains a meaningful and useful category for purposes of generic itemization. As for the best-known historical examples, along with the France of the Terror (always teetering between state and revolution), the list would include totalitarian states like Nazi Germany, the Soviet regime under Stalin, Maoist China, and Pol Pot's Cambodia; military dictatorships like Pinochet's Chile and Argentina following the coup of 1976; and, not least, religiously based states like Khomeini's Islamic republic in Iran. While diverse, they all fit the model of an extreme use of collective violence "combining large-scale killing with various forms of planned degradation of the human body and human dignity."[15] Adopting Arendt's thesis on totalitarianism, one could even maintain that they have in common a use of terror that, after being exerted against the opponents of the regime, goes on to menace practically the entire population, making all who are defenseless its target. Composed of arbitrary incarcerations, deportations, torture, executions, killings, and, not seldom, genocides—that is, in the last analysis, composed of violence centered on horror—such applied terror consists, on one hand, of the reduction of all defenseless citizens to potential victims and, on the other, of a system of control that forces them to inform on one another and even, through perverse ideological mechanisms, on themselves. The purge made famous by the Stalinist lexicon is emblematic in this sense. Similar in certain respects to the Virtue invoked by Robespierre, it bears witness to a violence understood as a regenerative force that entrusts terror with the task of purifying the political body of the internal enemy who is undermining its safety. Thus the Hobbesian theorem, which aimed at stability, is turned on its head, and the terror of the sovereign abandons its function of producing peace and security among its subjects, mutating into a sanguinary fury that overwhelms them or else into a continuous and general movement of purification that grinds down their lives. In this context, the individual need for security often turns into a symptom of hostility, whereas living under a daily threat to one's own existence appears as a sign of normality and fidelity. This explains why many of the regimes classified under the rubric "state terrorism" have a tendency to denounce precisely the security of daily living, or, if you like, well-being, as a sign of degeneration and corruption. It also explains why terrorism, in almost all its historical forms, including the form defined by Sartori as "global and faith-based," is profoundly at odds with modernity or, better, with a certain lifestyle, in an age when "lifestyles have globally become the central sign of moral style."[16] Terrorism in general, inasmuch as it makes violence into a destabilizing process, is indeed not aimed at guaranteeing a social order, as the Western political tradition, above all the modern state, would have it, but rather at spreading and perpetuating the order of terror. The defenseless person is not so much its easiest target, as is often said, as its necessary target.

This certainly holds good, with a few exceptions, for terrorism against the state, another category both debatable and highly articulated internally. Here I employ it merely to delineate the elementary difference between the use of terror by those at the top of the pyramid of institutional power, or formal public entities, and its use by individuals or groups, generally clandestine, who want to bring down whatever political form is in place. In the latter case, the list would have to include an array of terrorist formations so broad and heterogeneous as to create difficulty even for specialists in the work of classification. It suffices to mention the complex galaxy of anarchist groups, nationalist organizations advancing claims to autonomy (like ETA in Spain and the IRA in Northern Ireland), and politically inspired subversive organizations (like the Red Brigades in Italy or the Rote Armee Fraktion in Germany). Nor must we overlook the well-known situations in which recourse to terror arises out of the explosive overlap of territorial irredentism, questions of ethnic or national identity, and, last but not least, religious drives (the case in Palestine, Chechnya, and Kashmir). In the most violent scenarios of the modern world, like Afghanistan and Iraq, the long-standing and now globalized rivalry between Sunnis and Shiites, intersecting with intertribal struggles and fundamentalist ideologies, adds a notorious complication to the picture. Then there is the further dimension (already discussed) of linguistic difficulty: should these irregular combatants be called terrorists, or resisters, or insurgents, or revolutionaries? To resort to the lexicon of Schmitt, they comprise the figure of the "tellurian" partisan who fights against a real enemy but also the figure of the revolutionary partisan who is fighting an absolute enemy, transferring his acts of violence into an international or, as we say today, global space.

It is no accident, for that matter, that terrorism against the state often overlaps, and comes to coincide, with revolutionary terrorism. The latter, indeed, seems to be able to count on a structural ambivalence that not only allows it to inspire the actions of terrorist groups that attack the state but also makes it the initial phase of a sequence leading to the installation of a state terrorist regime; this is the case with the Russian Revolution. As noted above, the problem goes back to the French Revolution: already appreciated by many as a form of violence capable of overturning the ancien regime, it was valued even more by others, as a process that, while aiming to generate a new political form, ends by identifying itself, and above all finding its meaning, in the regenerative unstoppability of its own movement. It remains the case, to put it in Schmitt's terms once again, that the experience of revolution basically opens out into the international dimension, whereas the classic form of the state is based on territorial delimitation. So it is not surprising that the majority of terrorist organizations, even if originally engaged in local or national clashes that would justify labeling them as insurgents (and in certain cases, by their own self-definition, as revolutionaries), tend toward cooperation with other groups and the internationalization of terror. But when it comes to the capacity to overleap national boundaries and spread throughout the world, no vehicle displays greater potential than religion. The horizon of the international is replaced, in this case, by the universality that is typical of religions, particularly monotheistic religions, with their capacity to nourish "fanaticism," in the sense of "a movement of intransigent universalization."[17]

In this connection it should be noted that "religious concepts of cosmic war . . . are ultimately beyond historical control, even though they are identified with this-worldly struggles. A satanic enemy cannot be transformed; it can only be destroyed." The author of this remark also notes that, albeit without the clamor of the events of September 11, many "terrorists in the name of God" were bloodying the planet long before terrorism claiming affiliation with Islam took center stage.[18] In the opinion of some, center stage is in any case firmly held today by terrorists who see themselves not as the revolutionary vanguard of an oppressed people but as the vanguard of a community of believers (*umma*),[19] in other words, an armed minority that speaks in the name of a religious majority: the Muslims of the entire world.[20] Exterminating the defenseless in the name of religion and its fundamentalist aberrations has supplanted the pretense that it was licit to kill them in the name of Jacobin Virtue and the Revolution.[21]

For the purposes of a brief review of terrorism against the state, the best examples of the close connection between this phenomenon and the concept of revolution are the bombings by anarchists in the nineteenth century, especially when we consider the rapid process that led them to change the target of their exploits from political leaders and crowned heads to defenseless citizens. The bomb that exploded at the Liceo theater in Barcelona in 1893 is an emblematic example, as is the conviction repeatedly expressed by the authors of these massacres that there were no innocent victims because every citizen was an accomplice of the bourgeois state. Among the labels applied to the absolute enemy, "bourgeois" can in fact boast a certain primacy. As in the case, more recent and at the same time very ancient, of "infidel," we are dealing with a category that is broad, imprecise, and hard to determine, hence well suited to cover a multitude of helpless people. But in order to kill them, as Schmitt would say, what is needed is an idea in the name of which "no price is too high."

The linkage, structural and unbreakable, between terrorism and ideology is a decisive factor for the killing of the helpless. Not that we are dealing here with a linkage that concerns only anarchic violence or, more generally, violence on the part of groups classifiable under the category of terrorism against the state; as totalitarian regimes have shown, terrorism by the state feeds on ideology in an even more evident and basic way. Unlike that of totalitarian regimes, however, terrorism against the state, especially when it overlaps with revolutionary terrorism, cannot in general count on conventional channels of propaganda and the official machine of ideological indoctrination. Cultural organizations and educational institutions normally evade its control. As for the media, following the advent of the Internet and the globalized television networks of the digital age, the situation is obviously different. The propaganda function, for which the subversive groups of the past relied directly on the terrorist act itself and its effect on the nearby crowd, is implemented today by the diffusion and multiplication of the act through the media. It thus becomes, by definition and destination, a spectacular act. The spectacularized violence of Al-Qaeda bears atrocious witness to this, with its ability to exploit the "digital materiality of that online presence"—in the form of texts, demands, and proclamations—"that is the very substance of Al-Qaeda."[22] More generally, as research in this area indicates, many terrorist groups share the conviction that their massacres have an educative effect on the inert masses, awakening them into awareness of their oppression (variously read in political, ethnic, nationalist, identitarian, and religious terms) and spurring them to join the bombers, who see themselves as the vanguard and leadership, in bloody action. History has shown this claim to be unrealistic but, for just this reason, very indicative of the essential function that ideology performs in the construction of the absolute enemy as the target of worldwide aggressiveness.

Divorce from reality is a constitutive and well-known character of ideology. When it is married with terror, and even more when religion gives it substance, it has a tendency to simplify into a Manichaean logic that allows no gradations between the extremes of Good and Evil. Violence thus has no hesitation in putting itself in the service of the Good, specifically of a Good—or, if one prefers, a Truth—that even claims to benefit the victims, defenseless and random, of that very violence. It wasn't just bourgeois individuals who died when the anarchist bombs exploded, just as a striking number of good Muslims die in the massacres perpetrated by the various groups that identify themselves with True Islam: around sixty per day and sometimes as many as eighty in Baghdad at certain periods in 2005, when the clash between factions was most intense. But in the rhetoric of ideology, these are not tragic incidents or sorrowful losses, much less collateral damage, but the lucky chance, given to a few, to immolate themselves involuntarily for a cause they share, de jure if not de facto. This line of reasoning, typical of the combatant if not of the politician, entails the utilization of abstract categories made even more rigid by ideological simplification, in light of which the singular lives of human beings, all the more when they are defenseless, carry no weight. In the case of terrorist organizations with roots in communism, like the Red Brigades in Italy or the Rote Armee Fraktion in Germany in the 1970s and their "armed struggles," they tend not to perpetrate massacres, preferring to strike at specific individuals who are selected as symbols, representatives or "servants" of the "system." As shown by the Robespierrean prototype of a violence that mows down singular lives in the name of the goddess Reason, the resort to terror, without which Virtue is impotent,[23] is all the more effective when the range of its potential victims is as broad as possible. However paradoxical it may appear, to exterminate everyone, indiscriminately, constitutes the secret ideal of every terrorist program.

But only modern terrorism has succeeded in perfecting the model of an indiscriminate and global violence in which the everyone to be exterminated is synthesized into the anyone at all of the random victim. This, apart from anything else, is a good reason to sidestep the well-known problems arising from the use of the word "terrorism" and call it "horrorism" instead.

Horrorism is obviously nothing more than a name, and it is obviously vulnerable to the charge of oversimplification in comparison to the analyses, which are nothing if not extensive and articulated, supplied today by the various specialized readings of contemporary terrorism. Apart from highlighting the decisive influence of religious integrism and fanaticism, research on terrorism tends to offer a fairly complex picture, a mix of politics, economics, power struggles, individual ambition, and, last but not least, particular and capillary forms of ideological and military organization. That the topic is complex, precisely because of its novel and extraordinary dimension, is past doubt. That the factors listed above, and many others besides, with due emphasis on the importance of cultural humiliation,[24] contribute to this complexity is equally so. Particular emphasis should be placed (in the current context in which the classic model of the state is undergoing a process of disaggregation) on the explosion of terrorist acts that aim specifically to "produce" a different form of domination on a global scale. And even more emphasis should be placed on the fact that it is not civilizations that are clashing today, as Samuel Huntington suggests, but ideas, specifically ideas that claim to confer a pedagogic, punitive, and above all moral quality on the use of violence.[25] To adopt the viewpoint of the defenseless victims as a criterion, which leads me to use the term "horrorism," is not to dispute the results of specialized research on terrorism or to debate its theses but simply to look at the phenomenon from another perspective. From this perspective, today tragically plausible, horror appears more conspicuous than terror.

Can the same be said of the global terrorist, whom I am suggesting we call a horrorist? Is there not a risk that this neologism may hide his intimate relation to terror?

As generally delineated (adhering, as it were, to the protocols of classic terrorism), the terrorist sows terror but shields himself from it. To put it with more philological precision, he counts on the terrorizing effect of an act, unforeseen and unforeseeable, that aims to disperse violent death among others but does not personally risk it himself. Or, rather, he risks it in a certain sense through the unforeseen circumstances that every combatant has to allow for, but although he is ready to die, it is not his own death but that of others that is at stake at the exact moment of his use of terror. As a unilateral bearer of menace, he neither trembles nor flees, unlike his helpless victims. At least if the protocols apply. Because if not, if the violent death he gives to others were to entail his own as well, then, as the physics of terror guarantees, the terrorist would perhaps tremble too.

The hypothesis is not as futile as it might appear, much less incongruous. A discourse of this kind is commonly adopted to highlight what is termed the cowardice of the traditional terrorist act. It is asserted, not unreasonably, that to leave a ticking time bomb in a crowded place is not a brilliant example of courage. Yet the relations that courage has maintained, in other cultural contexts and various historical epochs, with the physics of terror ought to suggest a degree of caution. Although undoubtedly courageous, the warriors in Homer, including Hector, trembled and fled before the imminence of their own death. But subsequent literature, permeated with warlike rhetoric (whether patriotic or revolutionary) chose instead to make the person who looks his own murder in the face without blinking into the model of courage. The true combatant, such rhetoric assures us, never fears dying; terror does not stalk him. This ought to apply above all to today's suicide bomber, prepared to blow himself up along with his victims. The emblematic case of a violence immune to physics, he represents a specialist of terror who is immune to terror.

A decade before Carl Schmitt published his essay on the partisan, Ernst Jünger brought out a small book, apocalyptic in tone, entitled *Der Waldgang*. The figure of the Jüngerian rebel is not centered, like Schmitt's, on the enemy but instead on terror. Jünger's thesis is that the modern Leviathans, by which he means mass democracies or electoral dictatorships, enslave men by exploiting their fear of death. The rebel, the sole antagonist of the system, is precisely he who has no fear of dying. To conquer the fear of death "amounts to the overcoming of every other terror; they all have meaning only in relation to this basic question."[26] The rebel, says Jünger, is immune to the terrorizing apparatus of the state already theorized by Hobbes. He does not tremble for his own life, resists "zoological-political regimentation,"[27] and disdains the urge for security that the state machine uses to dominate citizens. As Jünger's text reveals, we are not dealing with a terrorist, much less a suicide bomber, but rather a figure who revives certain romantic traits of anarchism. It is no surprise that some aspects of this figure turn out to be highly serviceable for shedding light on the context of today's violence. On one hand, the strength of the Jüngerian rebel is grounded in his peculiar immunity to the physics of terror. On the other, he not only goes down the path that "leads to . . . sacrificial death or to the fate of him who falls in battle" but belongs above all to the ranks of those who "have died with confident certainty."[28] In Jünger's terms, this means that the rebel passes through the heart of the nihilistic mechanism but is not trapped in it—indeed, he crosses its line[29]—because he knows that every man is immortal and that "an eternal life has taken its place within him."[30] Imperviousness to the physics of terror, in the rebel, is thus nourished, in the last analysis and in anomalous terms, by a religious instance. It is precisely this instance that distinguishes the rebel from the criminal and justifies his acts of violence.[31] Terror has no purchase on him who does not believe that "in the moment when his fleeting presence dissolves, all comes to an end."[32] He has no fear of dying; indeed he makes available his own death in order to kill others in the name of a higher end.

A crucial element in Jünger's rebel prevents me from taking him as a horrorist ante litteram. Though he is committed to combat, his targets are the political and social apparatuses of domination, not defenseless people, or at least not exclusively. In this sense, his connections with today's suicide bombers are vague and distant. Yet a certain obsession with terror, interpreted in terms of an extraordinary immunity from its effects and a supraindividual mastery of violence, bears witness to a symptomatic affinity. On top of that, there is the thanatological penchant of an imaginary in which "the gates of the kingdom of the dead are thrown wide open and an abundance of gold pours forth."[33] Although the language is grounded in the worst rhetoric of the modern West, the worldwide stage for ontological crime on a vast scale is already prepared in Jünger's imaginary. Horrorism has already singled out the profile of its present champion.

# 15

■

## Suicidal Horrorism

*On the streets of Gaza, children play a game called shuhada,*
*which includes a mock funeral for a suicide bomber.*
—Jessica Stern, *Terror in the Name of God*

Among the many lexical problems arising out of the current debate
on terrorism, one is particularly curious. In order to indicate the
phenomenon of bombers who carry the explosive device on their
own bodies and detonate it in a crowded place, the European languages use disparate terms. In Italian, for example, we tend to use the
term *"kamikaze,"* borrowing the Japanese word that denoted one of
the squadrons of suicide pilots in the last phase of the Second World
War. The English language, responding to a descriptive exigency, prefers the expressions "suicide bombers" or "body bombers." The Italian
choice to adopt an analogy (even taking account of the use of airplanes in the massacre of September 11) is evidently incorrect, both on
the cultural plane and on that of linguistic contamination. But it does
lead to some interesting questions.

A comparison between the Japanese kamikaze and the actual suicide bombers claiming affiliation with Islam does in fact lead to results
worthy of note. One of these follows from the simple observation that
the Western vocabulary, starting with everyday language and the language of the media, doesn't behave in the same way when it comes to
names: right from the start, even at the time of the events, it accepted
the term "kamikaze," with which the Japanese pilots referred to themselves,[1] but continues to be impervious to the term *"shahid,"* which the
Islamic suicide bombers use to denote themselves. In the first case,
there is an immediate incorporation; in the second, a refusal that continues down to this day. As if the positive significance of both terms,

for those who use them to identify their suicidal actions, were unacceptable to the Western vocabulary solely in the case of the *shahid*.[2]

As Leonardo Sacco, the author of a book investigating this comparison, points out, "kamikaze" literally signifies "divine wind" and is an explicit reference to the storm winds that "preserved Japan from an almost certain invasion toward the end of the twelfth century by sinking the Mongol fleet."[3] In October 1944, with the American navy nearing the Philippines, the fate of Japan was just as much in the balance. As a last resort, a special corps of pilots was set up, assigned the task of smashing their airplanes, and themselves, into the enemy ships. Like the "divine wind" that destroyed the Mongol fleet, they were called upon to sweep away the American fleet and save the fatherland. Thus the word refers essentially to sentiments of nationalism. Even though tradition ascribed an origin to the Celestial Empire that was divine, like the wind that saved it, the kamikaze of the Second World War were not religious martyrs but national heroes whose glorious figure was, if anything, modeled on the abnegation of the samurai and the code of honor that prescribed ritual suicide. To sum up, in the context of Japan in 1944, the kamikaze is a loyal warrior who, in killing himself for the salvation of the fatherland, dies with honor.

"*Shahid*" on the other hand is a term that unequivocally alludes to a religious horizon. Like the Greek "*martus*," it denotes, in the Arabic language, both "martyrdom" and "bearing witness," more specifically he who bears witness to his own religious faith even through the sacrifice of his own life.[4] Although it concerns situations in which one is going to certain death, nevertheless this sacrifice does not have the character of suicide; neither, crucially, can it count on a culture and a tradition that view this extreme act in a positive light. The Koran, like the other Abrahamic monotheistic religions, condemns he who dies by his own hand to hell. On the plane of lexical choice, a much more problematic situation is thus created for today's *shahid* than was the case for the Japanese kamikaze. The term "*shahid*," applied to the suicide bombers, turns out to be improper and incorrect within the Muslim tradition, or, at any rate, it bends its lexicon to make it coincide with an act that that tradition unhesitatingly castigates. This explains, among other things, why the legitimation of the suicidal action carried out in the name of bearing witness and martyrdom, far from being taken at face value, as in Japanese society where ritual suicide was valorized, required the special intervention of religious authorities summoned to pronounce on the problem. These matters are obviously complex, as well as totally immersed by now in the messianic ideologies of destruction that characterize modern terrorism.[5] It is symptomatic, in any case, that the development of the doctrine called upon to legitimate suicide martyrdom in religious terms, as well as having to operate amid the rush of events, passes primarily through the recuperation of a conception of jihad—understood in the narrow sense of "holy war"—in which insistence on the sacrifice of life by those who, in fighting the infidels, bear witness to their faith is assuming ever more violent accents.

It is widely accepted that two events occurring at the start of the 1980s made a decisive contribution to this doctrinal development tending to the glorification of the *shahid* as suicide. One arose out of the Iran-Iraq war, during which the Ayatollah Khomeini decided to use adolescents as human detonators: their assignment was to walk across the Iraqi minefields and trigger the mines, thus opening the way for the Iranian troops. They strode forward to the cry of "Shahid! Shahid!" with the golden key of paradise suspended around their necks and a band containing verses from the Koran around their foreheads. From 1981 on, Khomeini enrolled around ten thousand of them, and the parents of the boys who got blown up were given a special "certificate of martyrdom."[6] This is not yet the full identification, in the technical sense, of martyrdom with suicide, but the scene already supplies those elements that will form part of the trappings, ritual and ideological, of the suicide bomber. What occurred on the scene of the second event was, however, much less ritualistic. It took place in Lebanon on 11 November 1982, when an extremist Shiite group from Hezbollah caused an automobile stuffed with dynamite to penetrate Israeli headquarters and explode, causing numerous deaths. In the driver's seat was a fifteen-year-old boy apparently unaware of the fact that the detonation would be triggered at a distance by remote control. Knowingly or not, he became "the symbol of the Lebanese resistance within a few years, and at the same time the forerunner of all the *shuhada.*"[7] At the turn of the 1980s the term "*shahid,*" which had been easily adapted to denote the boys who got blown up walking across minefields, thus came to denote boys who blew themselves up, turning themselves into bombs. Martyrdom was legitimated as a suicidal act and a homicidal act at the same time.

The kamikaze of the Second World War who dashed themselves into the enemy ships were obviously suicide homicides too. But there is a difference. Although perceived as "improper weapons" by the Western belligerents, they were soldiers who were killing other soldiers. Unlike the majority of today's *shahid*, their targets were not composed of defenseless victims.[8] That explains why, in specialized research, the Japanese suicide pilots are not included under the rubric of terrorism. It also explains why the term "kamikaze" could easily pass over into the occidental vocabulary, whereas the term "*shahid*" finds the door closed. In this sense, the incorrectness of the Italian language in calling the Islamic suicide bombers "kamikaze" is notable, whereas English appears much less incorrect in choosing a descriptive expression that, while revealing a reluctance to accept the name "martyrs" for those who immolate themselves in order to kill defenseless people, also avoids likening their gesture to that of the Japanese pilots. To register the fact that both are carrying out an act in which a suicide is at the same time a homicide is not in fact sufficient to reduce them to a single model, assimilating and blending them—unless we focus solely on the suicide that links them and ignore a decisive aspect of the homicide that distinguishes them.

Going by the news reports, the Western imaginary seems to be struck above all by the scandalousness of the suicidal act as a manifestation of disdain for human life, in particular for one's own. In the case of the Japanese kamikaze, relative to a time of war in which mass homicide was the rule and suicide an anomalous gesture, a reaction of this kind was, at bottom, justifiable. In the contemporary context, in which the anomaly ought to attach to the massacre of the defenseless rather than to the suicidal act, it is perhaps a little less so. Even today, though, appalled repugnance for a homicidal killer who kills himself prevails. The scandal is seen to lie in the aberrant, self-annihilating will of the perpetrator, despite the fact that the resultant slaughter of the innocent is starting to appear normal. Indeed, in the commentary on this matter, it is not uncommon to find appeals to the difference, a little stereotyped, between a West focused on the value of the individual life and an Eastern—or, better, orientalist[9]—culture supposedly predisposed to assign it little value. A framework of this kind was invoked, for that matter, with regard to the gesture of the Japanese suicide pilots, seen as contrasting with the spontaneous behavior of the soldier who, while knowingly risking his life and even taking part in missions from which he is not expected to return, still always hopes to come out alive somehow. Although it likes to celebrate the martyrdom of defenders of the fatherland,[10] the rhetoric of war in Western culture—Ernst Jünger included—shuns the celebration of suicide. Or at any rate does not celebrate it openly.

A famous example in this respect (not by chance an integral part of the schooling of children in Europe) might be the episode of Leonidas and the three hundred Spartans, who fell gloriously at Thermopylae while facing certain death but are not classified as suicides. More problematic with respect to the category of suicide is an episode that concerns a heroic martyr of patriotic Italian history. This was Pietro Micca, who in 1706 saved Turin from the French invaders by blowing up the tunnel leading into the city but was buried in the rubble himself on account of the short fuse he had knowingly lit. So, at least in the arena of war, especially patriotic war waged against a foreign occupying army, the figure of the martyr-suicide is not entirely unknown to the Western tradition, and a few aspects of the two cases mentioned are highly interesting. The story of Leonidas, when compared with a detail from the story of Pietro Micca, helps to bring an important point into focus. Whereas at Thermopylae they fought with swords, by the time of the scene that witnessed the sacrifice of the Italian patriot, modern science had put explosives at the disposal of the combatants. This changes the situation radically. Materials with high destructive potential—among them dynamite, invented by Nobel in 1866—have brought new instruments of death onto the scene, ones that, unlike the sword, lent themselves to the transformation of suicide into a deadly weapon whenever a body prepared to carry and detonate them was available.

In human history, bodies and war maintain a very complex relationship.[11] If it is true, to recall Clausewitz once again, that the essential relation between war and politics stands out in the Western tradition, the relation between the body and war is just as salient. We might in fact begin by emphasizing that, vis-à-vis the body, politics and war have contrasting attitudes. As the celebrated metaphor of the body politic reveals, politics has a predilection for a metaphorized body that extends to committees of "public health" and an endless gamut of "pathologies" and "therapies."[12] As the paintings of Goya document exemplarily, war, on the other hand, has to do with bodies of flesh and blood: living, warm, and pulsating or else transformed into cadavers. In general, from the viewpoint of the warrior, which obviously prevails here, these are the male bodies of combatants. Violent bodies for the most part, destined to be disfigured through a death just as violent. This is exactly the opposite of the disincarnate and conceptualized body—albeit always belonging to the male sex—that appears in the metaphor of the body politic. Italian once had a brutal expression for soldiers departing for the front: "*carne da macello*" (meat for butchering). As Homer knew, the theater of battle is a scene of butchery reserved for the bodies of warriors.

Not, it is worth pointing out, that bloody carnage is reserved for warriors and males in uniform alone. Women raped and killed, civilians run through, innocent people mortally wounded are all part of the homicidal violence of all wars, from Homer to our day, constituting its classic horrorist aspect. As for European history, until the First World War the battlefield on which soldiers clashed hand to hand, or at any rate fought with weapons at close quarters, remained the fulcrum of the scene of war. As already noted, with the progress of technology applied to the means of destruction, the picture changed rapidly during the course of the twentieth century. Bomb-carrying aircraft, guided missiles, and smart bombs, not to speak of the atomic bomb, not only enlarge and transform the field of battle, they display an irresistible tendency to drive the body of the warrior from the scene. The Gulf War of

1991, known to the news media as Desert Storm, is emblematic in this sense, when television, which transmitted the images live, bemused the spectator with strange fluorescent traces ending in dazzling splashes, from which the bodies of soldiers, like the bodies of the victims, were absent. That obviously did not mean that there were no bodies and that victims did not die by the thousands, gasping and bleeding. But it does mean that, seen with the eyes of the contemporary West, war is no longer a question of bodies but of advanced technology. Occupying the entire war scene and consigning it to the imaginary, the high-precision destructive machine, translated into digitized images, transforms the body of the warrior into a peripheral element of its mechanism, rendering it unworthy of media focus. When it does appear, it is in any case no longer a warring body made of muscles and flesh, of fear and fury, but rather a creature with robotic features and a mechanical pace. In a "post-heroic war" that no longer requires the tribute of blood and aspires to a "zero casualty option" for its robotized soldiers,[13] the engineering of devastation triumphs over bodies and swallows them up, concealing them.

This concealment also extends to the soldier's dead body when the corpse has been dressed for burial: today it is supposed to be absent, covered up, invisible. The public debate that arose following the unauthorized transmission of images of twenty coffins containing the bodies of soldiers killed in Iraq returning to American soil in April 2004 is well known. We are not dealing here just with a strategy regarding images that might undermine the morale of the country and the troops. The explanation lies rather in the imposition of an instance that Foucault has taught us to call biopolitics, reinforced by an ever closer intersection of economics and technology. Currently, in the Western world, the death of a soldier, while still described in terms of the sacrifice of a life, assumes a predominantly economic aspect. To the detriment that every army suffers from the loss of its soldiers, there is now added the calculation of the waste of the financial resources that were spent on training troops for technological war. Given that technology now makes it possible to kill without being killed, there is no longer any necessity to immolate the bodies of warriors.

## Scene

Paradigmatic in this respect is what happened on 14 January 2006 in the village of Damadola in Pakistan, where yet another extension of the "war on terror" begun by the United States in Afghanistan in October 2001 caused the deaths of eighteen people, all civilians, among them eight women and five babies. The American attack—following information, which later proved to be false, that one of the leaders of Al-Qaeda was hiding in the village—was carried out by unmanned aircraft armed with missiles. With no pilot onboard, indeed empty of bodies altogether, the aircraft were controlled from Nellis Air Force Base in Nevada, at a distance of thousands of kilometers from the site of the massacre. Inserted into a time of irregular and asymmetric warfare, a striking case of war horrorism that no rhetoric of collateral damage can obscure, this episode was a conspicuous example of decorporealized destructive technology. It shows that, in principle at least, the direct participation of the warrior in slaughter is avoidable

* * *

Even in the age of remote-control destruction, situations still arise in which the soldier must operate among troops on the ground. His eventual death thus tends to be taken as an accident, and an attempt is made to conceal its reality. Since, in line with biopolitical principle, technological war works to keep the body of the warrior alive, the corpse dressed for burial becomes a symptom of the impotence of the system. It falls under the same logic that, with respect to the scene of destruction, counts on the peripherality and invisibility of the living body as a guarantee that the soldier's body is extraneous to the purely technological reality of killing.

So it is no surprise that, in contrast, the destructive violence of the suicide bomber, conveyed by the body pure and simple, appears particularly scandalous. The explosives carried in a belt or a knapsack and even the detonation mechanism are unable to cast any technological shadow over the centrality of the homicidal body of the *shahid*. Biopolitics actually reverses its polarity here, throwing into relief a body that kills itself in order to kill others, as though the principle of keeping the warrior alive had turned into that of killing oneself. A radically biological version of thanatology emerges that, with sinister clarity, exalts the mortality of the body while at the same time making of the body itself a weapon of death. That this is a weapon, an explosive device, a low-cost smart bomb, especially from the point of view of the recruiters of the *shahid*, is something we should take literally. One of these recruiters, a member of Hamas, stated that "we utilize martyrs because we don't have the F16s, the Apaches, the tanks and missiles." Others, referring to Chechnya, depopulated by years of war, where women are more numerous than men, have specified that they are "the most plentiful and cheapest" weapon around.[14] "War technology incarnated" in low-cost bodies it may be,[15] but we are still dealing with an anomalous weapon. A perfect mirror image of the bodies of the American soldiers hidden from public view, this weapon, adopting a particularly macabre horrorist tactic, may even consist of an explosive device hidden inside a dead body. News reports from Baghdad regarding an explosion in January 2005 tell of an unusual explosive device stuffed inside a decapitated body, which blew up when the Iraqi police approached it to investigate.[16]

Leaving this lugubrious case aside, it is certain that a body capable of killing by killing itself seems not only scandalous but totally irregular, illegitimate, and above all unfair from the point of view of the technological imaginary of war today, which is still conceived by the official rhetoric of the West as an updated version of classic war. Nourished for years on the cold war scenario, for a long time the imaginary of the regular contemporary warrior foresaw attack by an opposing army in a symmetrical battle in which high-technology weapons of destruction would decide the outcome. But there is no symmetry between the war that the American and Russian powers, allies by now, are in a position to unleash and the strategy of suicide attacks; for that matter, there isn't even any battle. The growing, but not yet conspicuous,[17] phenomenon of the mere body ready to blow itself up anywhere renders empty not just the omnipotent dreams of military hypertechnology but the very concept of war that the regular combatants still maintain they are fighting.

# 16

**▬**

## When the Bomb Is a Woman's Body

*"I saw the head of a girl with long black hair in the middle of the street,"
Aaron Pinsker told Israeli television that Sunday, still trembling all over,
immediately after escaping the bomb blast. "I didn't recognize what
it was immediately. At first I thought it was a chicken or some other
animal, but when I looked closely I realized that it was a girl."*
—Stefanella Campana and Carla Reschia, *Quando l'orrore è donna*

"I have always dreamed of transforming myself into deadly shrapnel against the Zionists . . . and my joy will be complete when the parts of my body will fly in all directions," says young Reem al Rayashi in the video that records her last wishes, before the suicidal act that caused the death of three Israelis and wounded another twelve, among them four Palestinians. The mother of two children, twenty-one-year-old Reem blew herself up on 14 January 2004 at the Erez crossing, north of the Gaza strip.[1] She wasn't the first Palestinian woman to immolate herself in the bombings that followed the second Intifada. A few had done so already, and, among those whom Arafat enrolled in the "Army of Roses," others would follow her. But the fact that she identified her deadly weapon so clearly as the explosion of her own body renders her emblematic. In the imaginary of the young Palestinian mother, it is not the belt she wears under her clothing but her own body that explodes into a thousand lethal shards. Another who shared this conviction was Andaleed Khalil Takatka, another young woman, who, before her suicide bombing on 12 April 2002, in a crowded market in Jerusalem in which four Israelis and two Chinese lost their lives, asserted in the ritual video message that her "body is a keg of gunpowder that blows the enemy up."[2] The technology, even this rudimentary kind put together by hand, is eclipsed by the emergence into the foreground of the mere body as destructive material. Perhaps in this case, rather than corporeal material, it ought to be called carnal. As is typical of contemporary horrorism, the suicidal act consists of a mass killing that dismembers bodies and mixes those members up. In this sense, the English expression "body bomber" hits the mark. Bodies explode into pieces and become heaps of meat.

The first Palestinian woman to blow herself up was Wada Ifris, who immolated herself on 27 January 2002; she quickly became a national hero, her features reproduced in thousands of portraits that celebrated her martyrdom. In the sequence of suicide bombings committed by women, however, first place belongs to Lebanon, where in April 1985 Saana Mhayaleh died at the wheel of a car bomb. The list is long and geopolitically broad. It is estimated that among the Tamil Tigers of Sri Lanka, who come from the Hindu minority, 40 percent of those who commit suicide bombings are women, including Thenmuli Rajaratname, who became famous for killing the Indian prime minister, Rajiv Gandhi, in 1991. There have been examples of women acting as exploding bodies or living bombs among the Kurdish nationalist groups operating in Turkey; the country is now the target of armed Islamic extremism, as in the case of the bomber who caused a massacre at the Crocodile café in Ankara on 20 May 2003. Among the jihadist organizations of contemporary Iraq, two Iraqi women close to the unusual age of forty chose homicidal self-detonation on 4 April 2003. But the most disconcerting phenomenon concerns Chechen horrorism, which reserves this act to woman alone. The first, in June 2000, was seventeen-year-old Hava Bareva who, after making a video recording of her ritual testimony as a *shahid*, blew herself up in a car bomb which she drove at a government building, together with another girl who was only sixteen years old. With a certain regularity in the timing of the attacks, many other Chechen women followed her example; the phenomenon reached maximum intensity in 2004, when the explosion of two Tupolev aircraft in midair, causing ninety deaths, was attributed to four of them. The massacre in the Moscow subway, the work of a Chechen woman who carried the bomb in her purse, followed a few days later. After a short pause came the massacre at the school in Beslan in early September, in which women dressed in black with explosive belts were prominent among the hostage takers. This was the source of the name "black widows," prevalent today in media language. The best-known image of them, transmitted around the world by television, shows them lying lifeless on the seats of the Dubrovka theater in Moscow, which was occupied by Chechen nationalists in October 2002 and "liberated" by Russian military forces with poison gas that killed fifty of the hostage takers and 128 hostages. In this case, the belts did not explode (because, it appears, they were fake, although those wearing them did not know this), but the fact that the Chechen organizations assign the function of body bombers exclusively to women was finally displayed before the international community.

Among studies of the disturbing phenomenon of women who blow themselves up, there is a book, notable for its tone of indignation and compassion, by a young Russian journalist that focuses on the Chechen horrorists. Rather than "black widows," the title of the book calls them "brides of Allah,[3] because, in dying as martyrs, they supposedly celebrate their symbolic weddings. The author, Julija Juzik, states her intention of reacting to the scandal of female bodies that make themselves into instruments of death rather than sources of life and tries to understand the circumstances, the motivations, and the settings of such a repugnant gesture. The horror of the deed is repugnant in itself, apart from gender, as Juzik well knows. Yet in an Islamic culture, in which a woman "always stays in the background, timid and silent,"[4] it is inevitable that her making herself the protagonist of a public act of violence is particularly shocking. In the Chechen case, as in others of modern horrorism, any analysis that tries to understand the phenomenon must widen to include the historical, economic, and social conditions in which it arises and develops, as well as the daily scenario of violence and devastation around it. In this connection, there is often mention of desperation and, especially when it comes to the principal motive of the suicide bombings, of humiliation, as well as injustice and arrogance suffered for too long, of extreme choices on the part of those who have no other choice, and of mortified dignity that is compelled to redeem itself with a homicidal death. On the other hand, for reasons ever more tragically plausible, there is also talk of fanaticism and indoctrination, of manipulation of the young and exploitation of suffering. Yet a female body thrust into the foreground of the scene of violence, all the more when it is entrusted with the monopoly of homicidal self-conflagration, still remains particularly scandalous. No matter how important and exceptional the setting, no matter how serious and harsh the conditions in a Chechnya "thrown into turmoil by war, where roundups, summary killings, rapes, torture, violence, disappearance without a trace, and common graves, are the order of the day,"[5] the phenomenon has its own peculiarity that in the end confirms it as the most repugnant core of the contemporary horrorist picture.

As with other women who have studied the matter, for Julija Juzik to acknowledge the female face of today's horrorism is hard because it is so painful. It is easier to talk about a spreading homicidal violence in which the female body, torn away from the patriarchal curtain of its veils and consigned to mass murder, finds itself impotent and overwhelmed. In dealing with women who, especially in the case of Chechen society, play a weak and subaltern role, the temptation to identify them with the defenseless, exchanging their position for that of their victims, is indeed very strong. This stance is fairly frequent in modern writing by women dealing with the phenomenon of female suicide bombers. Though they do so in various ways and from different perspectives, the authors tend to sympathize with the objects of their investigations. "Sympathize" should naturally be understood here in the etymological sense of *sun-pathein*: to undergo or suffer together with the other. The underlying thesis is that the *shahid* do not act on their own initiative but are rather the victims of manipulation on the part of violent men who use them as pawns, exploiting the subordinate role of women in Islamic society. In the book *Army of Roses*, which is about Palestinian women suicide bombers, the American writer Barbara Victor notes, for example, that "it was never another woman who recruited the suicide bombers" and emphasizes the personal problems like widowhood, spinsterhood, sterility, or repudiation that "made their lives untenable within their own culture and society."[6] Stefanella Campana and Carla Reschia point out, for their part, that "like their male counterparts, and even more so, these women, whose stories are all alike, appear to have renounced, or been forced to renounce, every faculty of free choice, either with persuasion, or violence and the administration of drugs."[7] So it is easy to entertain "the suspicion that these Muslim women have no way out."[8] It is highly symptomatic in any case that, being women, the authors suffer to such an extent from the phenomenon of other women transformed into violent bodies that they view them as objects on whom suffering is inflicted rather than subjects of an active choice. In paradoxical fashion, the emphasis thus shifts from the helplessness of the victims to the helplessness of their assassins, even though the latter bear on their bodies, or rather make of their bodies, a weapon. Rather than the weapon that explodes, it is the body itself that is foregrounded—a female body that age-old tradition, both in the East and in the West, has always regarded as extraneous to the masculine realm of violence and historically destined to undergo it rather than perpetrate it. Added to that is the difficulty already mentioned of thinking of her as a body that takes life, against the background of an imaginary that thinks of woman as a body that gives life. The picture is, past all doubt, anomalous and disconcerting.

But not so disconcerting as to prevent us from remembering that Medea, and the series of infanticidal mothers that mark the long history of horror, are always there in the background and have evoked exceptional female violence for centuries. This obviously is not a warrant to see the female suicide bomber of our times as a new Medea, but Medea's gesture does make her surprisingly familiar to us. Her affinity with Medea holds good only up to a point, however, and can even be misleading. Media kills her own children. The women who blow themselves up today are not killing the flesh of their own flesh; they are spilling extraneous blood.

It is worth mentioning in this connection that, in today's debate on horrorist phenomena, the question of infanticide is sometimes touched on, although in crucially improper terms. A few of the body bombers were pregnant, and for that matter so were some of the women counted among the victims of the bombings. In these cases we ought to speak not of infanticide but of interruptions of pregnancy, onto which is projected, in distorted fashion, a notion of the female body understood as the maternal body par excellence. It is understandable for many reasons that the pregnant body shattered by the work of carnage is more bloodcurdling than any other and that it may represent the height of horrorism. But we are not dealing here with infanticide or with the paradigm of classic horrorism. The mask of Medea has a different story to tell. Medea, the infanticide, is not available to represent the violence, even self-inflicted, that befalls the pregnant mother. Medea kills her offspring when they are already born; she kills children, real living beings who incarnate, in the fragility of early life, a human vulnerability coinciding with absolute defenselessness. Medea, in sum, has nothing to do with a horrorist version of pregnancy. She does have to do with a violence against the defenseless that, through her figural potency, has been handed down for centuries as particularly female. This obviously does not mean that fathers do not murder their own offspring, much less that men do not murder children. But although the measureless terrain of male violence has given us many icons over the centuries, the fact that no infanticidal father has risen to the status of icon of child murder is something we cannot ignore. As the absolute icon of female violence, Medea is unique and is the most atrocious. There were reasons for myth to entrust the act, unexpected and yet foreseen, of the destruction of helpless ones to a woman, indeed to a mother. Every time that helpless ones are struck, wounded, killed—whatever the sex of the slayer—the ghost of Medea repeats her gesture on the renewed scene of horror. When the slayer is a woman, and especially a mother, whom we would expect to be a caregiver, the scene becomes more intense, drawing nearer to the essential nucleus of horror. It is thus of less importance that Muslim women, ready to immolate themselves and probably unaware of the Greek myth, are driven by desperation or humiliation or indoctrination or fanatical manipulation. In the act of killing the defenseless, they are Medea once again, or at any rate it is the gesture of Medea that we, the cultural daughters of that myth, suffer yet again in their murderous deed.

The legend recounts how Medea killed her sons to get revenge on Jason, an ungrateful and unfaithful husband. The infanticidal women we read about in the newspapers generally have more obscure motives, which psychoanalysis undertakes to explore. The primeval sense of horror does not reside, in any case, in their motives or in the impulses of a disturbed uncon-scious, much less in reasons that, no matter how unjustifiable and execrable, locate violence within the logic of means and ends. As supreme violence against the absolutely helpless, the horror resides entirely in the act itself. It is the actualized scene—often mistaken for ritual and cynically consigned to aestheticization—upon which is reiterated the destruction of the defense-less. Although it is a reaction of the stomach and the gut, the disgust that such a scene provokes is rooted in an ontological dimension in which the distinction between mind and body no longer counts or perhaps, as with children, does not count yet. That explains, in passing, why women who write about the phenomenon of female suicide bombers tend to emphasize the reasons and circumstances that supposedly make them into helpless vic-tims, forced to immolate themselves, rather than intentional mass murder-ers. Seen from a compassionate female perspective, the suicide of the help-less, the self-destruction of the vulnerable, tends, in this case, to foreground the paradox of a weakened Medea who turns her violence against herself. As though, occupying both poles of the murder, the woman were redoubling her role of victim, and it were someone else's role to answer for the atrocity of the deed—in this case, the male clan that dominates and crushes her.

But to answer for one's own actions, especially on the horrorist scene, is the responsibility of her who carries them out. In this sense too, Medea is a precious icon. Her killing of her own sons, known to her by name and loved in their unrepeatable singularity, contrasts, in a highly instructive fashion, with the utterly anonymous killings of today's descent from the classic para-digm of horror into the abyss of horrorism. The ontological crime commit-ted upon the defenseless today has a double face. The defenseless person who is killed, indeed butchered, is robbed of the dignity of his or her irre-mediably singular being. The bomber, male or female, on the other hand, leaves behind a trace of himself or herself, in a testament recorded on video, and counts on the immortalization of his or her own name. In this connec-tion, there has even been talk of an organization of violence that supposedly allows women, *in articulo mortis* at any rate, to emancipate themselves from their subaltern position by inscribing themselves as protagonists in the political history of their communities. But, far from making them equal to men, their deed ultimately makes even more evident the contradictions that are rooted in their gender identity. Emancipation in violence not only reverses the stereotype of the female, making it even more pronounced; it fails to cancel, indeed it highlights, the female peculiarity of an act of destruction directed at helpless victims.

When compared to the story of Medea, this forced reading in an emanci-patory key ends by highlighting yet another important aspect of the phenomenon. Although there is no shortage of politicized interpretations of the myth of Medea, her gesture is carried out in the domestic realm and is emblematic of an order that we might call family centered and even, with a certain anachronism, private. The act of infanticide as such, especially when carried out by a mother, necessarily bears this stamp: it is, so to speak, a family crime. To the extent that the killing of the defenseless at female hands is today a renewal of the crime of Medea, its movement into the political sphere and the valorization of it as a gesture of political militancy bring about, on the symbolic plane at least, a reversal of meaning. According to the emancipatory thesis, such crimes allow Muslim women to escape from their traditional domestic servitude and rise unexpectedly to the status of heroines of the community, taking on a political role. But even on the symbolic plane, the difficulties multiply, beginning with an imaginary that continues to privilege the maternal figure in these women, making their status as combatants into a factitious, if not utterly cynical and cruel, facade. There is not much doubt about this. To judge by all the relevant literature, both in the culture to which today's female suicide bombers belong and in the so-called Western world, it is always, without exception, the question of the maternal figure that comes to the surface. Given that, on top of the trauma of a woman who kills defenseless beings, there is the scandal of the transposition of this murder from the private sphere into the public one, indeed into a global media spotlight, any attempt to justify the act is forced to engage in insincere and artificial argumentative acrobatics. How could it be otherwise? Whatever the emancipatory or military value assigned to it, the female body that explodes in order to rip apart innocent bodies is always, symbolically, a maternal body. The crime of which it makes itself the protagonist has ontological roots, sunk deep in the human condition of vulnerability, that no political pretext can expunge.

Medea kills her sons, but unlike other female masks in Greek tragedy, she doesn't kill herself. To kill herself along with them would not have allowed her time to gauge the depth of the crime she has committed and to take responsibility for it. In contrast, the instant of time that blows the bodies of the "human bombs" and their victims to pieces today annuls the dimension of time: time in which to face up to the reality of one's own crime and to answer for it singularly. Closed in on itself, suicidal horrorism thus takes pride in the unappealability of its work in the service of an instantaneous and irresponsible violence. In this sense, it is no surprise that books on female suicide bombers written by women who are disposed to understand them, if not justify and sympathize with them, have a tendency to minimize the ethical responsibility of the bombers. The effort to portray them as victims, as passive instruments with no way out, fits precisely into this framework. Nor is it surprising that the great majority of such books prefer the form of biographical narrative, reconstructing various singular lives so as to identify, in each, the factors of conditioning or misfortune that have led, practically inevitably, to such a devastating outcome. The dignity of a personal history is thus piteously restored to these unhappy women, albeit at the cost of an ethical absolution that reverses the sign of the guilty irresponsibility inscribed in the horrorist deed.

## Story

Among the many relevant stories we can read, one is really unforgettable. It tells of two sixteen-year-old girls: the Palestinian Ayat al-Akhras and the Israeli Rachel Levy, who was born in California.[9] Both were brunettes with long hair. When they entered the Supersol supermarket on the outskirts of Jerusalem together on 29 March 2002, some took them for sisters, although they did not know each other. Ayat was wearing an explosive belt studded with steel nails and screws to make it more deadly. Stopped by the security guard, who may have intended to search her, she detonated it near the entrance. The effect was devastating, and many people were injured, but, according to the news broadcasts on the radio, the number of dead was, fortunately, small. According to the first count, in fact, there were "only" two victims: Ayat herself and the security guard, a man of fifty-two. Actually Rachel too was among the dead, but the pieces of her body at the site and the resemblance between the two girls led the investigators to suppose that all the female remains belonged to the body of Ayat. The least damaged of these, in any case, was taken to be hers: a severed head with beautiful features and long black hair.

It was Rachel's mother, watching the news on television, who recognized, in this bloody *meduseion*, the face of her daughter. "I realized after watching the news reports and seeing the photograph of the suicide bomber that she resembled my daughter. I knew that somehow they had confused Rachel with the other girl and the body they had was my daughter's." She went down to the morgue to identify the body formally. "Her face was beautiful, not a mark on it. It was her body that had been destroyed."

In recounting this atrocious story, Barbara Victor interweaves the two life stories and insists on the strange destiny that brought them together by chance, as though they were two interchangeable girls whose lives were cut short by the history of the Israeli-Palestinian conflict. The relatives of both had the same reaction: the disaster took them by surprise, and they lapsed into profound consternation. But one neighbor of Ayat's did not conceal a feeling of pride: "How many children and innocent people have the Israelis killed?" he asked, adding, "This is a natural response. The equation works both ways." This is one opinion among many, but the logic to which it appeals is well known and surfaces in many documents and interviews. It is an aberrant logic, in which the slaughter of innocents becomes a criterion that justifies, indeed demands, the slaughter of other innocents. The criterion of the warrior thus recedes into the background, confirming that today it is no longer the concept of war that holds the field. Nor is the reference to children to be understood, here and elsewhere, as rhetorical artifice or pathetic exaggeration. Far from killing them by mistake, horrorism actually prefers children, because in them it finds the perfect victims. The vulnerable par excellence, in fact the absolutely defenseless, they restore to today's horror its originary stamp and transmit its destructive message more effectively than any other victim.

# 17

## Female Torturers Grinning at the Camera

*It is not accidental that in the torturers' idiom the room in which the brutality occurs was called the "production room" in the Philippines, the "cinema room" in South Vietnam, and the "blue lit stage" in Chile: built on these repeated acts of display and having as its purpose the production of a fantastic illusion of power, torture is a grotesque piece of compensatory drama.*
—Elaine Scarry, *The Body in Pain*

In the contemporary repertoire of horrorism at the hands of women, the female torturers at Abu Ghraib occupy a special place. The attempt to pass them off as victims themselves is a very difficult feat to perform, although a series of attenuating circumstances is often invoked, including a perverse effect of the movement toward emancipation or the influence of a certain kind of social and cultural conditioning in the American hinterland. Although the debate provoked by the events of Abu Ghraib is vast and multivocal, two fundamental topics for reflection stand out within it. Some commentators, while emphasizing the scandal of torture perpetrated by women, have tried to tie it to the more general scandal of the illicit use of torture on the part of those who are supposed to represent the model of democratic legality and the culture of rights. Others, focusing on the role of photographs and images in the whole affair, have preferred to raise the problem of the obscene and the way it has become a media spectacle in the era of the Internet and digital technology. In the end, though, these two topics overlap, revealing the true nucleus of the question. The blood-curdling peculiarity of the events of Abu Ghraib has precisely to do with the anomalous overlap between spectacle and torture. In its historical phenomenology, from the trials of the Inquisition to the third degree in a modern police precinct, interrogatory torture is constitutively a practice hidden from public view. But another form of violence against the helpless, well known in former times, was visible and indeed spectacular: painful public torment, normally ending in death (*supplicium* in Latin, *supplice* in French, *supplizio* in Italian). As Foucault was aware, there is an essential difference between them.

In *Discipline and Punish*, he notes that the ceremony of the *supplice*, an exhibition of physical injury horrendously inflicted and offered to the crowd, disappeared from Europe and the United States at the beginning of the nineteenth century. In the space of a few decades, the economy of punishment changed drastically, going from spectacular violence upon "the body . . . as the ultimate object of . . . punitive action" to a less barbarous and "more human" system aimed at reeducating the convict, or rather his "soul," with a view to reinserting him into society.[1] From the scaffold at the center of the square, we move to the disciplining rationality of the prison. This change, Foucault notes, not only involves the complex network of judicial and carceral knowledges but also concerns the forms of politics of which it is an expression. This is the period that sees the definitive decline of the absolute power of kings and the establishment of the modern democracies. Justice and penal law are now conceived around a citizen endowed with rights, among which stands out the right not to be subjected to corporal humiliation, punishment, and degradation, especially in public. Even capital punishment becomes an act that takes life but in theory avoids physical suffering as well as personal degradation.

In classic criminal law, however, the *supplice* aims at calculated physical torment far exceeding what would be needed to cause the death of the convict. Among the most atrocious figures of horrorism, it relies on "the art of maintaining life in pain, by subdividing it into a 'thousand deaths,' by achieving before life ceases 'the most exquisite agonies.' "[2] Its political function is to display to the populace an invincible force that, through violence upon the body of the criminal, restores the sovereignty of the king, "manifesting it at its most spectacular."[3] The punishment is carried out, writes Foucault, "in such a way as to give the spectacle not of measure, but of imbalance and excess; in this liturgy of punishment, there must be an emphatic affirmation of power and of [the] intrinsic superiority" of the sovereign.[4] This explains why the *supplice* must be public and visible, indeed prominently exhibited before the subjects. And it also explains why the violence that precedes it, the torture of which it is the outcome, has to take place in hidden quarters and remain invisible. Far from manifesting the king's invincible force on the public square, torture was actually a routine part of penal procedure, a precise technique for investigating the truth of the crime in order to yield a just sentence. There is neither spectacle nor revenge in interrogatory torture, merely an application of the technology of pain to force the guilty party to confess.

The invisibility of interrogatory torture is an important element for Foucault. Although it, like the *supplice*, consists of savage violence inflicted unilaterally upon helpless persons, torture demands secrecy. "The entire criminal procedure, right up to the sentence, remained secret; that is to say, opaque, not only to the public but also to the accused himself."[5] Both are horrorist scenes centered on the body of the victim, but torture aims at a confession, whereas the *supplice* is based on humiliation and revenge. Both, moreover, albeit in different ways, aim not to kill but to cause suffering. As a practice for ascertaining the truth and delivering the self-confessed criminal to public punishment, torture had to keep the "patient" from dying during the procedure; indeed, medical expertise about the technology of the various *tormenta* (devices for inflicting pain) was employed so as to prevent "cases of decease during the work."[6] The *supplice*, on the other hand, does aim to end his life—but not too soon. The "policy of terror," as Foucault calls it, aiming "to make everyone aware, through the body of the criminal, of the unrestrained presence of the sovereign,"[7] delights in unfolding at a slow pace. So slow and atrocious, working on the body to delay its death, that not even the howl of Medusa would seem adequate to evoke it. During the rite of the *supplice*, which could last as long as two weeks, it was usual for the body, still alive, to be dismembered, sometimes even quartered: pulled apart by four horses attached to the limbs of the convict and driven in different directions, dragging his arms and legs with them. Often melted lead was poured into the wounds of the victim, and sometimes the torturer would cut open his belly and throw his innards on the fire as he watched. This public butchery had an array of tools for traumatizing the flesh: knives, hatchets, axes, irons, and pincers. "The infinitesimal destruction of the body is linked here with spectacle: each piece is placed on display. . . . In the same horror, the crime had to be manifested and annulled."[8] Thus does the sovereign's vengeance assert the disymmetry of power and put it on show for the crowd. It is precisely a political instance of superiority that drives the horror of the *supplice*. Expressing the potency of a king who can erect, here on earth, "the theater of hell," the public splendor of the scaffold concludes the secret work of torture.

Foucault does specify, albeit in passing, that the torture of the past "was not the unrestrained torture of modern interrogations; it was certainly cruel, but not savage."[9] It was, in other words, and apart from its well-known atrocity, a well-defined procedure, legal and regular. It did not take place in secret because it was illegal. On the contrary. It was hidden from public gaze precisely because that was what the law stipulated. In late modernity, the logic has been reversed. Although the new political model sees the disappearance of the *supplice*, the same is not true as regards torture and its constitutive secrecy. But now it is the illegality of their actions that forces the torturers to operate in secret. Equipped with instruments that have kept pace with the development of technology, they torture in their secret rooms on behalf of a sovereign who knows about it, indeed who sometimes commands it, but cannot admit it publicly. The juridical scene becomes uncertain and confused. While the law does prohibit torture, debates tellingly arise on the boundary that separates it from harsh interrogation aimed at ascertaining the truth about the crime. Some propose legalizing torture in cases in which the information thus obtained might, as they say, save many lives and guarantee public safety.[10] For a society based on guarantees and rights, however, such a hypothesis is traumatic and is rarely defended frankly. Amid general hypocrisy, therefore, governments resort to the expedient of transporting the accused to a country that still practices torture and is prepared to interrogate prisoners on behalf of third parties.

Still practiced virtually everywhere around the globe, torture is today covered over with hypocrisy, cynicism, and pretense in the nations that hold aloft the torch of rights and align themselves under the civilizing banner of the West. In this sense, the themes discussed by Foucault in the first part of *Discipline and Punish* can supply the modern West with fundamental food for thought and even a few good arguments for differentiating itself from contemporary societies in which, through stoning or the amputation of a hand, as well as decapitation with a sword in the middle of the square, the horror of the public *supplice* lives on. But precisely here lies the (Foucauldian) problem: when it comes to torture, the difference is much less easy to assert. From the standpoint of a realistic analysis, without hypocrisy, it arouses no surprise that in the prison of Abu Ghraib, already a theater of horrors under the regime of Saddam Hussein, the Americans too tortured prisoners.

Although it may seem paradoxical, even the worldwide visibility that the torture in Abu Ghraib finally achieved is not really surprising, given the circumstances. Although perpetrated in secret rooms, the actions of the torturers were in fact programmatically aimed, as regards both ends and means, at the realm of the eye. The setting not only did not prohibit photography, it allowed for and utilized it: both as an official tool of documentation for the Pentagon archives and above all as an instrument of humiliation for the victims. The threat that photos depicting them in humiliating positions would be shown to the relatives of the torturees formed part of the torture and was one of its fundamental instruments. The art of the digitized image—a technology born for the Web and destined for the Web—was recommended and encouraged at Abu Ghraib. Far from being an unforeseen contingency, the "souvenir photos," in their wretched banality, were just one of the variables, inevitable because embedded in the overall strategy, of the operations that were under way.

As we know all too well, these photographs feature two women in clumsy, artificial poses, gazing at the lens with a smile, or rather a leer, on their faces. The fact that they were women rather than men was one of the requirements of those who staged the whole scenario of degradation, experts on the subject who were specifically consulted. Lynndie England, who was working in an accounting office in the prison administration at Abu Ghraib, was promoted to her new position as torturer by these very experts for the purpose of "showing the prisoners hell." For men particularly sensitive to any insult to their virility, as is the case in Arab culture, to be tortured by women is a supplementary humiliation, calibrated "with skill so as to affront sensitivities and taboos rooted in the imaginary of the Islamic male."[11] What's more, these women were untrained actresses of little talent, who emphasized the caricature of female perversion and moreover of precisely the sort of perversion that Islamist fanaticism tends to ascribe to Western women. Atrocious enough on its own, the practice of torture in the rooms at Abu Ghraib thus multiplied and heightened its impact. The scene was, to begin with, structurally twofold. There was the event, nude and crude, of violence against the victims, and there was the digital technology that reproduced it in images. The female torturers alternated between mimicking torture and the real thing; indeed, they adapted the real torture inflicted on the bodies and minds of their prisoners to the torture they were pretending to inflict for the camera. Nor did this amateurish and crudely derisive piece of playacting fail to include a few "citations" of the best-known images from the modern history of horror. The shot of the hooded prisoner with his arms extended as if on a cross was evidently quoting the misdeeds of the Ku Klux Klan made famous by the American archives of racist crime. The dogs on leashes, baring their teeth and snarling threateningly at the prisoners are, for their part, a clear reference to the Nazi concentration-camp universe. Then there is a batch of obscene photographs (reportedly the largest portion) that draws on the most vulgar album of cheap mass pornography. In this case—which according to leaked reports about the unpublished images includes forced masturbation, simulated homosexual intercourse, and sodomization—the female protagonists are obviously all the more de rigueur. Adhering to male fantasies of perversion, or perhaps sharing them, the female torturers impersonate the sadistic dominatrix who sexually humiliates the male. The latter, however, is, ambiguously, on this militarized scene, the *other*: the enemy to be offended and devirilized, who vicariously gives his female and male torturers sexual pleasure.

Even if saomasochistic culture plays a part, sexual pleasure is perhaps an inappropriate term here. The photos do not convey the idea of carnal ecstasy (although there is arousal) but rather that of an obtuse and grotesque form

of diversion, witless and trivial. What stands out in them is a spectral caricature of torture reduced to the level of filthy farce. Phantasmic copies of real
torturers known to history, the Abu Ghraib tormentors and their victims
appear as specters, personified citations of horror, grotesque mimes from a
gallery of infamy. Torture in this case, materially perpetrated on bodies but
no longer concealed, indeed acted out for that worldwide audience that the
Internet guarantees, becomes spectacle. You could even say that it becomes
*supplice*, except that it lacks any trace of the old splendor on which Foucault
lays such stress. The Latin verb *"spicere"* (which means "to see" and is the
etymological root of both "spectacle" and "specter") actually exerts pressure
here in the direction of the farsical and the parodic. Reanimated by the horrorist rite,[12] sovereignty no longer manifests itself as an invincible force but
rather as the presence of an institutionalized power on whose "dirty" complicity the actors in the amateur theater of violence can count. The (accidental) unmasking of the illegality of the torture thus pales before the (substantial) self-revelation of a system that seems to be able to reproduce the
*supplice* only in the form of caricature. They tortured us "like it was theater
for them," said one of the Abu Ghraib detainees during the U.S. court mar-
tial that investigated the abuse a few months after.[13] This court-martial,
along with other official investigations and numerous public declarations,
all provided support for the theory that the guilty soldiers were "a few bad
apples," a theory obviously aimed at shifting blame away from the upper levels of the military and political leadership involved. It is more likely that the
photographs of Abu Ghraib, far from denouncing abuse on the part of a few
insubordinate and perverted soldiers, actually reveal the presence of a more
widespread and profound evil. What we have here, in substance, is a particular version of the banality of evil produced by a society of spectacle that
habitually covers its horrorist deeds with hypocrisy while at the same time
blurring the line between pretense and reality. In a certain sense, confirming the classic linkage between politics and lying,[14] the events in the Iraqi
prison bear witness that, in the current relationship of the West with violence, it is the realm of the fictitious that triumphs. The symmetry is almost
perfect: the political leadership lied about the presence of weapons of mass
destruction in Iraq and displayed faked photographs of them to legitimate
the bombing, and the torturers were in the habit of miming for the camera
the torture that they were inflicting in fact.

In a 1985 book reflecting on bodily suffering, Elaine Scarry points out
that torture "goes on to deny, to falsify, the reality of the very thing it has
itself objectified by a perceptual shift which converts the vision of suffering
into the wholly illusory but, to the torturers and the regime they represent,
wholly convincing spectacle of power."[15] So if there is something peculiar

and intensely horrendous in the scene of Abu Ghraib, it doesn't have to do with the usual presence of the fictitious but with a will to emphasize and exceed it. For the element of speciousness structurally characteristic of torture is here exasperated beyond all measure. Yet that does not mean that the representation of power expressed on this scene becomes less convincing. Rather, making excess its just measure, the portrait verges on perfection. The global public gains access to the self-representative theater of the *arcana imperii*.

No matter how inevitable—indeed inscribed in the digital technology that formed part of the torture—it was, the publication of the images from Abu Ghraib was nevertheless an accident. In the sequence of events, this accident occurred at the end of April 2004 when several journalistic investigations came into possession of the photographs and made them public, revealing the Pentagon cover-up. The launch of the operation, which immediately spread them around the world thanks to the Internet, was famously due to *The New Yorker* and the television program *60 Minutes*. Although a number of men perform their roles as torturers with enthusiasm in these photos, it was the grotesque poses of Lynndie England and Sabrina Harman that immediately gained the media spotlight. That the scandal concerned primarily the female protagonists was confirmed by the sex of the general in charge of the prison, Janis Karpinski. Public opinion, especially the feminist sector, was thus compelled to acknowledge that the horror of Abu Ghraib is all the more disgraceful in that the scene is crowded with women. From a certain point of view, which appeals to women's relational aptitude and not just to the redemptive altruism of their traditional stereotype, this was a symbolic catastrophe.[16] In most feminist commentary, however, emphasis falls on the perverse outcome of an emancipatory process that, in admitting women into the military, makes them, on one hand, equal to men in the exercise of violence but continues, on the other, to force them into a subordinate and instrumental position. Lynndie and Sabrina, it is said, were obeying their superiors, adapting to the horrorist culture of their environment. The torturers' defense, that they were compelled to follow orders (the typical position that, in the case of Eichmann, allowed Arendt to speak of "the banality of evil") seemed in effect to corroborate the idea of this subordinate role. But if we do want to invoke the category of "banality of evil" for the events of Abu Ghraib, as many have, the question is substantially different. What is banal here is above all the stupidity of a criminal act committed in the excitement of farce. Good girls from the American heartland, Lynndie England and Sabrina Harman were its miserable mimes. Striking helpless prisoners, they were simultaneously mimicking the savage violence of the soldier giving vent to his brutality, the same brute's obscene fantasies about sadistic women, and, last but not least, an utterly female cruelty incarnated in a few perverse reprises of the Furies already known to history. The list in this regard is fairly long, although not to be compared to that featuring men over the millennia. It includes, for example, Hildegard Lächert, the Austrian torturer who distinguished herself through atrocities against children in the Nazi Lager at Majdanek, or more recently Pauline Nyiramasuhuko, the Rwandan woman of Hutu origin who, during the slaughter of the Tutsi in the "machete war," encouraged the militias to "rape the women before killing them."[17] Moving from history to fiction, it is very likely that pornographic portrayals of sadistic women and female torturers in films and comic books were the ones most accessible and familiar to Lynndie England and Sabrina Harman. Obviously, cultural circumstances favor the adoption of models within one's own reach.

It is well established, in any case, that the female presence on the horrorist scene of torture and murder is not in the least a novelty confined to the scandal of Abu Ghraib. What is new here, though, and therefore all the more criminal, is their taste for duplicating violence against helpless victims in their abominable farce. In this sense, if one really wants to insist on the centrality of the women in the whole business, the torture at Abu Ghraib, transformed thanks to the media into a caricature of the *supplice*, has also degraded the symbolic density of the tragedy of Medea, reducing it to a dumb, vulgar comedy. That this was a comedy aimed at valorizing the pathetic talent of the actresses, though as yet unaware of their future role as celebrities, is evident: on the set, the women torturers expose their faces with satisfaction, winking at the camera, so that the digital image will preserve and transmit them. In this sense, they add an ulterior aspect to the savagery of Nazi torture, in which "both for perpetrators and for spectators, the humiliation, harassment, and killing of victims provided a distraction and source of amusement."[18] At Abu Ghraib the singularity that gave itself up to the immortalizing mission of digital technology was proud of itself. The same cannot be said, however, for the victims who appear on this scene. Mostly forced into the primal humiliation of nudity, they are anonymous bodies, often photographed from behind or with hoods on their heads in order to cancel the singularity of their faces. It is their penises or their buttocks that stand out: obscene parts, depersonalized and generic. Nude bodies, piled up into a pyramid, that become limbs—parts. Worse than death— as the victims themselves stated and as the horrorist practice of torture typically is—the humiliation consisted of a dehumanization at the hands of the director, who, in the frame of the shots, intentionally covered the facial features of uniqueness and annulled them. What emerges is the perfect accord of these images with those of the lacerated faces nevertheless perceived by now "as elements of an anonymous mass" or as generic collateral damage in a war that has correctly been defined as faceless.[19]

There is something barbaric and inhuman in torture, a profound violation of ontological dignity, which the images from Abu Ghraib have helped to identify as extreme crime, distinguishable from every other kind of violence, cruelty, and degradation. In torture the asymmetry of power emerges as absolute: "the victim is in a position of complete vulnerability and exposure, the torturer in one of perfect control and inscrutability."[20] In this sense, torture is an intensely malign form of human relationship, its most radical perversion. Not just because the torture victim, stripped of all autonomy, is forced to participate or "collaborate" in the mechanism of his suffering but above all because the victim, in his relationship with his torturer, is here a vulnerable person held in place and unilaterally exposed only to *vulnus*.[21] The other, the torturer, wounds him and is there only to wound him. There is no alternative or reciprocity. There is no way out, only the infinite and prolonged repetition of unilateral suffering.

The official investigations and judicial proceedings following the scandal of the Abu Ghraib photographs have tried, as everyone knows, to promote the thesis that the essence of the misdeed lay in the sadistic and deviant behavior of a few of the soldiers involved, a handful of "bad apples."[22] Corroborating the classic connection between politics and lying, this has not only confirmed a deeply rooted tendency of the U.S. authorities to engage in dissembling behavior but has obviously helped to supply new matter for modern reflection on torture,[23] compelling the critical literature on the matter to bring its own arguments up to date. Special emphasis has thus been placed on "interrogational torture,"[24] that is, on the difference that supposedly separates harsh but legal interrogation techniques from the degeneration of these techniques into torture. The task of extracting information from the victims, or, if one prefers, making them confess the truth, belongs for that matter to the traditional paradigm of torture illustrated by Foucault. Obviously though, for analyzing the facts of Abu Ghraib today, things are more complicated: once you allow legal practices intended to make the prisoner suffer in mind and body, perhaps even listing them in detail in dedicated manuals and thus recommending them, to distinguish between harsh interrogation and interrogational torture often amounts to no more than abstruse and ghastly quibbling.[25] Nor do things become any simpler when it comes to the second type of torture discussed in the literature on the subject, terroristic torture, by which is meant a technology of pain intended to frighten and intimidate both the victims who actually undergo it and their accomplices and supporters. Cutting loose from the pretended legality of the interrogational model, the discourse here passes over not only into the realm of intimidation but into that of revenge and humiliation, which allude symptomatically to the *supplice*. And yet we are always, even in terms of frank horrorism, within the domain of rational, or at any rate strategic, behavior, in the domain of violent acts that appear to select their own ends or rather pretend to do so.[26] As though to torture rather than simply kill served some useful purpose. As though a certain utility—information in the case of interrogational torture; intimidation, humiliation, or revenge in the case of terroristic torture—were the upshot.

That utility played any fundamental part in the atrocious theater of Abu Ghraib is, however, doubtful. Most of them bit players, 90 percent of the detainees in the Iraqi prison "were of no intelligence value"[27] according to the assessment of the American authorities themselves, in other words were of no utility when it came to supplying information. As for intimidation, revenge, and humiliation, the torture certainly included them among its goals and drew nourishment from them for its own cruelty, yet not in such a way as to assign these objectives a decisive role and make them the pivot of a strategic economy. As the photographs demonstrate, what prevailed was the pleasure of farce, the entertainment of a horror transformed into caricature, a license to dehumanize on the part of willing actors in an atrocious pantomime. In this sense, in the contemporary era and in the global spotlight of history, the viewpoint of the regular fighter—in regulation uniform and endowed with regular horrorist "appetites"—achieved its most expressive portrait at Abu Ghraib. In an age in which the traditional figure of the enemy has been definitively replaced by the defenseless as casual victim, the traditional figure of the warrior has also promptly adapted to the general festival of violence against the defenseless by making way for an obscene caricature of itself.

To compare the incomparable, you could even say that, after the images from Abu Ghraib, what has emerged is a contrast between the actors of a violence against the helpless who show that they accompany their crime with a certain trivial enjoyment and the actors on the other side who reveal a propensity for the grim and the lugubrious, even though they sometimes hymn the joys of paradise as the reward for slaughter. But in this respect, the phenomenology of contemporary horrorism is so complex in the array of its modes, attitudes, and tones as to discourage any reductive contrast. The very disconcerting fact remains that Abu Ghraib presented horror in the imbecile and idiotic form of the leer. As though, having lost even the howl that freezes in her throat, all that remained of Medusa today were a dull repugnance.

# Appendix

■

## The Horror! The Horror! Rereading Conrad

There is a specific literary genre that requires a foray, at least, in a book of reflections on horror. One might peruse Poe and Lovecraft and, after that, perhaps, turn one's attention to the horror genre in the cinema. But for many reasons it is above all Joseph Conrad who supplies interesting material on the topic of horrorism, starting with those famous words "The horror! The horror!" that form the last enigmatic whisper of the dying Kurtz in a crucial passage from *Heart of Darkness*. A true laboratory, in which modernity can take a critical look at itself and its own violent machine of expansion and domination, the novel is also receptive to an intensely political reading. Hannah Arendt confirms this, defining it as "the most illuminating work on actual race experience in Africa."[1] She sees it as an account of the marriage between "race and bureaucracy" that, after its advent in the age of colonial imperialism, went on to crystallize into the system of totalitarian horror. So does Francis Ford Coppola, who, in his celebrated *Apocalypse Now* of 1979, rereads Conrad's masterpiece in cinematic terms, setting it amid the horrors of the war in Vietnam. Nor is there space here to cite the extensive critical literature that continues to reread the novel in political terms, activating interpretive modules that are various and often clashing. From whatever vantage point, *Heart of Darkness* is now recognized as a classic of horrorism by contemporary thought on violence, which it evidently has the merit of narrating in an extreme form that exceeds war, murder, and cruelty. It is also a reminder of an ontological crime in which the West cannot avoid seeing itself mirrored.

The West traverses the story in many directions and assumes diverse, often ambiguous figures, which render it legible from varying, if not opposed, points of view. The sequence of events is, however, essentially simple. Hired by a commercial organization simply known as "the Company," Marlow travels up the Congo river aboard a steamboat until he reaches the station where he meets Kurtz—a first-class agent about whom disquieting rumors are circulating—"in the true ivory-country."[2] Delirious and ill, Kurtz is demented by now, and in this sense the voyage is a trajectory that advances into the folly of colonial exploitation in Africa, into "the merry dance of death and trade" that European imperialism imposes on the black continent. But the same trajectory also has a reverse movement, in which the West or, rather, its so-called civilizing mission goes deeper into the darkness of its own heart and is forced to recognize it. With the emphasis placed on the usual opposition between darkness and light—here obsessively utilized and recurring—the Enlightenment protocol is reversed, confirming itself as the historiographic model of a comprehension whose "constitutive" superiority nevertheless tolerates self-emendation or self-problematization.[3] The retelling of Marlow's experience seems in fact to suggest that the primitive darkness of the African land, into which the progress of the white man advances claiming to shed light, is in truth something that lies at the very origin of that progress and remains and indeed is exalted there. Testimony to this comes above all from the "culminating point" of this experience, Kurtz, in whose delirious figure savage violence and civilizing violence seem to coincide perfectly. Adored as a god by the "brutes" who surround him, he represents a West that has regressed to the dark matter that generated it and still gives it substance. Precisely for this reason, Kurtz is the man best suited to speak its name, as though it were the last residue of an act of supreme cognizance, emitting "a cry that was no more than a breath." These are the famous words: "The horror! The horror!" Albeit definitive, the utterance is opaque, but, as the narrator says, it seems "to throw a kind of light" on the whole meaning of the tale.

There is, in Conrad's story, a gaze upon Africa "with Western eyes" if not an outright racial prejudice,[4] which Hannah Arendt's reading risks reinforcing. According to Arendt's thesis, Conrad's lesson lies in his having demonstrated that the lives of indigenous peoples—obscure shapes who move nimbly and randomly against the dark rim of the forest, shadows of shadows, evanescent specters—constitute "a world of infinite possibilities for crimes committed in the spirit of play, for the combination of horror and laughter."[5] A "mass of naked, breathing, quivering, bronze bodies," busy "like ants," the savages would thus have the essential function of revealing the horrorist impulse that characterizes the colonizers. In Arendtian terms, this signifies that the inhabitants of the jungle appear to the Europeans as inhuman—if not, indeed, superfluous—beings, the killing of whom is like the crushing of a mosquito. But the horror, according to Arendt, lies not just in the crime that follows upon the perception of this inhumanity but, more subtly, in the intuition on the part of the colonizers that it is all too human. As Marlow confesses, the suspicion inexorably insinuates itself into the agent of civilization who travels back up into the darkness of the jungle that he is voyaging "in the night of first ages" populated by prehistoric men with whose brute humanity he still has a "remote kinship." "No, they were not inhuman," Marlow confesses, adding, "you know, that was the worst of it— this suspicion of their not being inhuman."[6] Africa as the prehistory of Europe, savage nature as the distant past of civilization, in other words, darkness as the "originary stage" in which the white man is forced to recognize himself and back to which, in the emblematic case of Kurtz, he is ready to regress,[7] thus delineate one of the main axes of the tale. It is perhaps the weakest axis, understandably disposed to fracture in the face of the senselessness and enormity of a crime that Conrad punctually denounces, impeding the narrative from resolving itself around a definitive nucleus.[8] Yet to the extent that it orients the story's events, weaving it around the relation between "whites" and "savages," it does end by suggesting that, although the horror of this crime is *ours*, we ultimately share the roots of it with *them*. An aggravating circumstance of considerable weight is thus added to the charge sheet against the colonial rapine. As Conrad himself, yielding to a somewhat stereotypical vision, seems to maintain, their nature as "brutes," still immersed in the pure vitality of the ferocious primordial world, actually renders them innocent, whereas our own civilized ferocity, cynically conscious of its atrocities, translates the same violence into guilt.

When Marlow approaches Kurtz's house for the first time, he sees that it is surrounded by a symbolic circle of "heads drying on . . . stakes under [the] windows." Although habituated by now to experiences that make "the usual sense of commonplace, deadly danger" comforting, he is disconcerted by the sight but notes that "after all, that was only a savage sight, while I seemed at one bound to have been transported into some lightless region of subtle horrors, where pure, uncomplicated savagery was a positive relief, being something that had a right to exist—obviously—in the sunshine." So, according to Marlow, in the display of the decapitated heads there is still a horror that is innocent because natural and savage but rendered criminal by the white man, who engrosses it in a world of more subtle horrors. We are dealing, at bottom, with the same primitive horror that draws Kurtz into its abyss, "by the awakening of forgotten and brutal instincts, by the memory of gratified and monstrous passions." At the beginning of human history, in

the night of primordial ages that the indigenous people still inhabit—
Conrad seems to say to us—there lies a natural impulsion to massacre that
can only reveal itself fully as crime in the violence of the civilized man who
has suddenly come into contact with the brutality of the primordials. The
recommendation to "Exterminate all the brutes!", the conclusion Kurtz
reaches in the report commissioned from him by the "International Society
for the Suppression of Savage Customs," thus has a highly ambiguous, as
well as paradoxical, valence. In a certain sense, it seems to be directed at
everyone: at both the brutes who are still immersed in the innocent ferocity
of the natural world and the agents of progress who have transformed this
ferocity into organized brutality. In the experience of Marlow, the explorer
of the colonial universe, there is salvation for neither the former nor the latter. Tragically nihilistic because dedicated to the horror that supposedly
characterizes the human species seen through Western eyes, *Heart of Darkness* opens onto a void or, as the (telling) expression goes in Italian, onto *un
orrido* (a deep and gloomy gorge).

*Under Western Eyes* is the title of another famous work by Conrad. It is
one of his two political novels (the other is *The Secret Agent*) that abandon
exotic scenarios and adventures on the sea and take as their subject anarchic
and revolutionary terrorism in Europe. Interest thus shifts to a horrorist
theater more—so to speak—classic and familiar. It is well known that Conrad, whom critics often accuse of conservatism, furnishes very hostile
descriptions and disdainful judgments of subversive groups. These two novels supply ample evidence of this, albeit within the usual narrative machinery that distances and conceals the author.

*Under Western Eyes*—the beginning of which recounts an assassination
in freezing Petersburg at the hands of a student—has as its background the
plotting of revolutionary groups, shot through with anarchic populism and
nihilistic ideas, who oppose czarist despotism. Conrad narrates, in Dos-
toyevskian tones, the betrayal of the assassin by another student, Razumov,
and the events that lead the latter to operate as a secret agent for the Russian
government amid the revolutionary emigré community in Geneva. An infil-
trator and reluctant hero of a double game, he judges the subversives from
his uncomfortable position and vents, through Conrad's pen, his cynical
contempt for them. Razumov defines them as "poisonous plants which
flourish in the world of conspirators, like evil mushrooms in a dark cellar."[9]
Among these, the character of Nikita is described with particularly lugubrious sarcasm; his sinister alliterative nickname, Necator, is well suited to a
man who "was supposed to have killed more gendarmes and police agents
than any revolutionist living." Razumov, the voice of conscience in the story,
has a propensity in any case to suppose that every Russian student capable

of succumbing to "the self-deception of a criminal idealist" is an "imbecile victim of revolutionary propaganda, some foolish slave of foreign, subversive ideals." Nor does he refrain from passing judgment on a category that plays a decisive role in the political lexicon of modernity, the common people. "They are brutes," he exclaims during a difficult conversation with Peter Ivanovich, the "great exile" who guides the revolutionary plotting from Geneva, and he adds: "as far as that goes, a brute is sound enough . . . and you can't deny the natural innocence of a brute." Revealing the hidden hand of the author, the tonality thus becomes, for a brief narrative interlude, decidedly Conradian. In this case too, it is the naturalness of the brutes that guarantees their innocence. This, in the land of Russia and in accord with a celebrated literary tradition, amounts to suggesting not only that the people are the only sound heart of the nation but above all that this soundness contrasts with the despotic criminality and subversive violence wielded by a civilized horde of government bureaucrats and subversive intellectuals.

The Secret Agent deals with a spy—obviously—but the novel is set amid the intrigues of anarchist London and thronged with grotesque characters; in describing them, Conrad expresses even more openly his hostility toward the violence and ideology of radical groups. But it is not this aspect that makes the novel valuable for exploring the theme of horrorism.

The Secret Agent narrates the strange and pathetic story of a helpless person who explodes with his bomb. Published in 1907, the novel was inspired by a dynamite attack that actually took place in London in 1894. The event had captured public attention both because of its purpose—to blow up the Greenwich Observatory—and because of the belief that an agent provocateur was pulling strings throughout the whole affair. In Conrad's novelized version, the agent provocateur is in fact the protagonist. We are not dealing here with an enigmatic or satanic figure but with an indolent and mediocre man who is not even productive as a spy for the Russian embassy in the anarchist circles of the capital and is forced to instigate a terrorist act in order to justify his salary. Like his comrades in London anarchism, whom he frequents and "organizes," Verloc is a tragicomic character, inept and grotesque. In order to carry out his mission, the best he can manage is to assign the bombing to a poor retarded boy, the young and inoffensive Stevie, who is also his brother-in-law and lives under the same roof as him. Easily manipulable, innocent, and quite unwitting, the boy has the task of leaving the ticking bomb in the Greenwich Observatory. But things work out differently. While crossing the park, Stevie trips and falls, causing the bomb to explode and blow his body into a thousand pieces with no damage to the building or anyone else. Highlighted, in Conrad's plot, by the strategic uselessness of the deed, horror thus emerges into the foreground and occupies the center of the tale.

The detailed description of this horror falls in the novel to the Chief Inspector: "Blown to small bits: limbs, gravel, clothing, bones, splinters—all mixed up together. I tell you they had to fetch a shovel to gather him up with."[10] The scene replays in Verloc's mind with the same blood-curdling detail: "after a rainlike fall of mangled limbs the decapitated head of Stevie lingered suspended alone, and fading out slowly like the last star of a pyrotechnic display." In other passages as well, in which the boy's body becomes "an accumulation of raw material for a cannibal feast," a "heap of mixed things, which seemed to have been collected in shambles and rag shops," Conrad continues to emphasize the repugnant details of the event. Indeed, the accumulation of disgust signals a decisive turn in the story. Constructed around this turn, the story in fact suggests that the death of Stevie is not just an involuntary murder, a tragic incident, a sinister fatality. It is not even the foreseeable result of Verloc's vile and irresponsible schemes. Rather, it becomes the paradigm of the ontological insult inherent in the dismemberment of a helpless person, whose absolute vulnerability is here purposely thrown into relief by the boy's mental retardation and idiocy. Harmless, trusting in the good intentions of the person manipulating him, needing care and protection, Stevie is, in the last analysis, a child or, rather, *the* child. In this sense, he is the exemplary vehicle of the narrative process that will reveal the horrorist nucleus of the supposedly terrorist basis of the bombing. Apparently dedicated to the theme of terrorism, the narrative development intersects both perspectives and compares them. All the atrocious inconsistency of the strategy of terror, already recounted in the early chapters concerning the London anarchist group, is finally unmasked by the pure horror that, from the outset, has nourished it.

Critics have often pointed out the pathetic, if not ridiculous, side of these Conradian anarchists, rootless and eccentric, who gather around the tragicomic character of Verloc. It is plausible that Conrad makes them strikingly stupid, frantic, and presumptuous precisely in order to emphasize the material horror nestled within their nihilistic lucubrations. Toothless old Yundt exemplifies this when, happy to proclaim himself a terrorist, he confesses that he dreams of a group of men "strong enough to give themselves frankly the name of destroyers . . . no pity for anything on earth, including themselves, and death enlisted for good and all in the service of humanity." The Professor, whom Conrad characterizes as "the unwholesome-looking little moral agent of destruction," does so even more. He actually fears that the mass of humanity, in whose name he claims to act and whom he sees as a swarm of locusts, driven by the force and potency of nature, may be "impervious to sentiment, to logic, to terror too perhaps." Apart from the resistance of the masses to logic, the most "dreadful" doubt that assails the Professor is that the immense crowd of humanity may be "impervious to fear." The physics of terror, meaning the effect on which the strategy of destruction, of which he is the apostle, is counting, would be nullified if that were the case, leaving destruction as the sole reality of the operation, the unique meaning of the act and the design behind it. A professional of terror and inclined to reflect on the new world he wants to mold, the moral agent of destruction is crucially perturbed by the thought that his profession has no purpose outside itself. If terror is ineffective, unproductive, useless for masses immune to its effects, the circle closes viciously. All that remains is mere destruction and the humanity that it selects as its object. In the guise of such an object, Stevie thus appears as a perfect victim. He is actually at the same time the agent and the instrument of the violence that destroys him, being moreover, in all the roles he unconsciously plays, completely trapped in the circularity of the destructive act that, in disintegrating his body, finally and tragically makes explicit the stamp of horror the governs the entire operation.

If doubt and introspection dominate in *Under Western Eyes*, there is, in *The Secret Agent*, a political critique of terrorism conveyed by the portrait of the terrorist as the agent of a destruction that is an end in itself. One of the minor characters in Dostoyevsky's *The Possessed* has already stated sarcastically, "It is suggested to us . . . that we should unite and form groups with the sole object of bringing about universal destruction."[11] The two novels are obviously incomparable in style and profundity, but Conrad too deserves recognition for his ability to grasp the self-referential valence of a destructive project that transforms its own means into its own ends. In Arendtian terms, we are thus faced with a terror that has lost its purpose or, rather, has become its own true purpose. Taking on a gratuitous character, violence short-circuits and vents itself on the indistinct and indifferent "mass of humanity," coherently insensitive to the proclaimed political goals that are by now external to the violence. The figure of Stevie—an involuntary body bomber ante litteram—can represent the core of this logic precisely inasmuch as he lends his innocent existence to the self-referentiality of the destruction that he involuntarily embodies. What makes him an exemplary victim and not an accidental martyr is precisely his innocence, that paradigmatic status of helpless creatureliness that allows him to disclose the horrorist substance of the act carried out unintentionally. The young Alfred Hitchcock errs therefore when he makes Stevie in his film *Sabotage* (a free adaptation of *The Secret Agent*) a bright and enterprising lad unaffected by mental retardation although reduced to being an unwitting instrument of the dynamite plot. The innocence that makes Stevie an exemplary victim is actually all the more emblematic the more the boy, in his state of eternal infancy, is constitutively defenseless and vulnerable. He not only knows nothing about the event; he would not even be capable of understanding or imagining it. In choosing him as the instrument of horrorist destruction, Verloc basically counts on this very factor.

It is worth emphasizing that the paradigmatic innocence of Stevie has both an ethical and an intellectual valence. An eternal child, he is not only excluded by definition from the realm of responsibility and guilt; he does not know what he is doing because his mental retardation—and not casual, or arranged, innocence—prevents him from understanding it. In other words, the horror of which he is the involuntary protagonist escapes him even as the possible object of a cognitive faculty he does not possess. There are, for that matter, many ways to know one's own crime or, rather, to make the act of one's own crime coincide with full and transparent awareness of it. Apathetic, cynical, and distracted, Verloc is not an outstanding champion in this regard. It is not he who brings out, through contrast, the absolute innocence of Stevie. When it comes to horrorist violence, in order to find such a champion—in command of a destruction that is carried out in an aware manner and that assumes the status of object of perfect cognizance, indeed of apposite science—we have to leave Conrad's writings behind and advance past the tragic turn of the century. Certain intense degrees of violence against the helpless, combined with a drive to discover its effects in order to strengthen and control it, only come about after Auschwitz. In the cinema, a 1977 film by Ingmar Bergman is particularly significant in this respect. Set in Berlin in the early 1920s, *The Serpent's Egg* reconstructs the dark atmosphere that presages the horror of the Nazi Lager as an experimental laboratory for the study and modification of the "human species." Among the characters is a certain Doctor Vergerus, probably a double of the infamous Mengele, competent in physical and psychological torture of every kind and, above all, a specialist in forcing human guinea pigs to commit suicide through the administration of pain. Responsible for a secret program of experiments that already anticipate a social model soon to prevail, he not only inflicts infernal suffering on his helpless victims but, in the name of science, observes, studies, and catalogs them. Indeed, so pure is his interest in scientific knowledge that, at the moment at which he must commit suicide with poison to avoid capture, he is pleased to observe his own death in the mirror and dictate a medical description of the symptoms into a recording device. The dimension of knowledge, applied to the perfecting of murderous technologies with respect to which it has the status of end rather than means, thus rises to absolute fullness and total control: nothing escapes it, not even the experience of the "scientific" agent of destruction who undertakes, willingly and with full coherence, to serve as both subject and object of the horrorist act about which he vaunts professional expertise. Champion of a dehumanization that is definitely sliding toward biopolitics, integrating himself into his own experiment, Doctor Vergerus succeeds in becoming the last of the samples held under his cognitive observation.

In Vergerus, author of a murderous plan that surpasses the meaning of murder, there is a way of killing himself that goes well beyond the meaning of suicide. Analogously, although at the opposite extreme of the horrorist scale and not by his own will, Stevie becomes the agent of a murderous plan that for him turns into suicide without his having the capacity to understand the meaning of either. Poles of an extreme divarication, Conrad's moving character and Bergman's ignoble one seem to share the function of expressing the senselessness of the self-referential short circuit that nestles in the substance of horrorism—always with the proviso that we are dealing here with two diametrically opposed perspectives. In the case of the retarded boy, called upon to represent the paradox of an absolute innocence, the scene of combined homicide and suicide is entirely summed up in the figure of the defenseless victim. In the case of the Nazi doctor, called upon to represent the paradox of a crime that aims at its own absolute scientific transparency, the scene is entirely summed up in the figure of the murderer. For the rest, there is no need here to press the comparison beyond its textual and temporal limits, forcing the different languages of the two authors into the straitjacket of analogy. Albeit on the restricted plane of fiction, Stevie and Vergerus belong to profoundly different worlds and allude to different cultural contexts. Yet both seem able figuratively to evoke that excess of meaning—one might say, that repugnance of the concept with respect to the enormity of the ontological crime—that reveals the peculiarity of horror and distinguishes it from the phenomenology of terror. As though, in this theater of violence, one's own death and the deaths of others were not the true stakes in the game. Or as though the history of destruction had need of images and names that, renouncing the simplicity of murder, would impel it toward other spirals of meaning.

# Notes

## Introduction

1. John Collins and Ross Glover, eds., *Collateral Language: A User's Guide to America's New War* (New York: New York University Press, 2002). See especially Roberto Cagliero's preface to the Italian edition: *Linguaggio collaterale* (Verona: Ombre corte, 2006), pp. 7–17.
2. See François Heisbourg, *Hyperterrorisme, la nouvelle guerre* (Paris: O. Jacob, 2003).
3. See Giovanni De Luna, *Il corpo del nemico ucciso* (Turin: Einaudi, 2006), p. xv.

## 1. Etymologies: "Terror"

1. See the entry *"tremo"* in P. Chantraine, *Dictionnaire étymologique de la langue grecque: Histoire des mots* (Paris: Klincksieck, 1984).
2. Ibid., s.v. *"phobos."*
3. "Fuyard, déserteur" appear in Chantraine (see n. 1), while "runaway" is supplied by H. G. Liddell and R. Scott, *A Greek-English Lexicon* (Oxford: Clarendon, 1968), s.v. *"treo"* in both cases.

## 2. Etymologies: "Horror"

1. See the entry *"horreo"* in E. Ernout and A. Meillet, *Dictionnaire étymologique de la langue latine: Histoire des mots* (Paris: Klincksieck, 1985).

2. See Károly Kérenyi, *The Gods of the Greeks*, trans. Norman Cameron (London: Thames and Hudson, 1951), pp. 48ff.

3. Julija Juzik, *Le fidanzate di Allah* [The brides of Allah], intro. Roberta Freudiani (Rome: Manifestolibri, 2004), p. 29. [The name of the author, a Russian journalist, is transliterated in various ways; in the German edition of her book, it appears as Julia Jusik. There is apparently no English translation. Extracts from it appearing here are translated into English from the Italian. WM]

## 3. On War

1. Carl Schmitt, *The Concept of the Political*, expanded ed., trans. and ed. George Schwab, foreword Tracy B. Strong (Chicago: University of Chicago Press, 2007), p. 33.

2. Carl von Clausewitz, *On War*, trans. and ed. Michael Howard and Peter Paret (1976; rev. ed., Princeton: Princeton University Press, 1984), bk. 1, chap. 1, sec. 2, p. 75.

3. Pindar *Nemean Odes* 4.33.

4. Nicole Loraux, *The Experiences of Tiresias: The Feminine and the Greek Man*, trans. Paula Wissing (Princeton: Princeton University Press, 1995), pp. 91ff.

5. Rachel Bespaloff, *On the Iliad*, trans. Mary McCarthy, intro. Hermann Broch (New York: Pantheon, 1948), pp. 99, 47.

6. *Iliad* 20.46.

7. Loraux, *The Experiences of Tiresias*, p. 77.

8. Here I wish especially to cite Giovanni De Luna's book *Il corpo del nemico ucciso* (Turin: Einaudi, 2006), with which I find myself strongly in sympathy. It seems to me that we are both trying to look at war from an unusual perspective, in his case, that of the bodies of the dead, in other words the treatment given to the body of one's enemy, or friend, whereas in my case the focus is on the helpless victim. To know war historically starting from the dead who represent its sole final concrete product, writes De Luna, "is like looking at the grass from the position of the roots; the methodological perspective changes, but so do the conceptual priorities and the content" (p. xvi). Reading De Luna's book, which I did when my own work was almost finished, unexpectedly relieved my sense of fatigue, especially when he voices his "profound unease" with an analysis that attempts to control, with the detachment of an interpretive hypothesis, material so repugnant and atrocious. It is hard to speak about things that make one fall numb or perhaps scream.

9. *Iliad* 24.347.

10. Loraux, *The Experiences of Tiresias*, p. 96.

11. Ibid.

12. On this, a fundamental work is still Charles Segal, *The Theme of the Mutilation of the Corpse in the Iliad* (Leiden: Brill, 1972).

13. *Iliad* 5.738–743.

14. Bruno Snell, *The Discovery of the Mind: The Greek Origins of European Thought*, trans. T. G. Rosenmeyer (New York: Harper and Row, 1960), p. 21.
15. Hesiod *Theogony*, l. 933. For an interpretation of the Hesiodic passage with reference to the theme of terrorism, see Umberto Curi, "Alle radici del terrore," in *Iride* 46 (2005): 465ff.

# 4. The Howl of Medusa

1. "Le visage du vivant, dans la singularité de ses traits" (Jean Pierre Vernant, *La mort dans les yeux: Figures de l'autre en Grèce ancienne. Artémis, Gorgo* [Paris: Hachette, 1985], pp. 47–48).
2. "Quand vous dévisagez Gorgô, c'est elle qui fait de vous ce miroir où en vous transformant en pierre elle mire sa terrible face et se reconnaît elle-même dans le double" (ibid., p. 82). See also Linda Napolitano Valditara, *Lo sguardo nel buio* (Rome: Laterza, 1994), pp. 61–64.
3. This thesis is advanced in the 1922 essay "Medusa's Head," the English version of which appears in vol. 18 (1920–1922) of *The Standard Edition of the Complete Psychological Works of Sigmund Freud*, trans. James Strachey et al. (London: Hogarth, 1955–), pp. 273–274.
4. Thalia Feldman, "Gorgo and the Origins of Fear," *Arion* 4 (1965): 487ff.
5. See John Freccero, "On Dante's Medusa," in *The Medusa Reader*, ed. Marjorie Garber and Nancy J. Vickers (New York: Routledge, 2003), p. 114.
6. I have reflected on this theme in my book *For More than One Voice: Toward a Philosophy of Vocal Expression*, trans. Paul A. Kottman (Stanford, Calif.: Stanford University Press, 2005), originally published as *À più voci: Filosofia dell'espressione vocale* (Milan: Feltrinelli, 2003).

# 5. The Vulnerability of the Helpless

1. Arendt developed the theme of uniqueness as exposure principally in *The Human Condition* (1958; 2d ed., intro. Margaret Canovan [Chicago: University of Chicago Press, 1998]). I have dedicated a series of reflections to this theme over the last decade that flow into the thesis I am putting forward here; see *Relating Narratives: Storytelling and selfhood*, trans. Paul A. Kottman (New York: Routledge, 2000), originally published as *Tu che mi guardi, tu che mi racconti* (Milan: Feltrinelli, 1997); and *For More than One Voice: Toward a Philosophy of Vocal Expression*, trans. Paul A. Kottman (Stanford, Calif.: Stanford University Press, 2005), originally published as *À più voci: Filosofia dell'espressione vocale* (Milan: Feltrinelli, 2003).
2. Judith Butler, *Precarious Life: The Powers of Mourning and Violence* (London: Verso, 2004), p. xi.
3. Ibid., p. 19.

4. Ibid., p. 30.
5. Ibid.
6. Ibid., p. 41.
7. Ibid., p. 44.
8. Alasdair MacIntyre, *Dependent Rational Animals: Why Human Beings Need the Virtues* (Chicago: Open Court, 1999), p. 1.
9. Butler, *Precarious Life*, p. 45.
10. Ibid., p. 28.
11. Ibid., p. 31.
12. Judith Butler, *Giving an Account of Oneself* (New York: Fordham University Press, 2005), p. 70. Although she does not press the issue of vulnerability in this work (of notable critical density), Butler does investigate further the relational dimension of the "I."
13. Thomas Hobbes, *Leviathan*, 2.20; *On the Citizen*, 9.1–7; *The Elements of Law, Natural and Politic*, chap. 23 (= pt. 2, chap. 4), 1–8.
14. Thomas Hobbes, *The Elements of Law, Natural and Politic: Part I, Human Nature, Part II, De corpore politico; with Three Lives*, ed. J. C. A. Gaskin (Oxford: Oxford University Press, 1999), chap. 23 (= pt. 2, chap. 4), sec. 3, pp. 130–131.
15. Thomas Hobbes, *On the Citizen*, trans. and ed. Richard Tuck and Michael Silverthorne (New York: Cambridge University Press, 1998), 8.1, p. 102.

# 6. The Crime of Medea

1. See Maria Grazia Ciani, introduction to the Italian translation of Euripides, *Medea*, trans. and ed. Davide Susanetti (Venice: Marsilio, 2002), p. 16.
2. In the context of a political and feminist interpretation of the entire story in *Medea: A Modern Retelling*, trans. John Cullen (New York: Nan A. Talese, 1998), Christa Wolf proposes a modern rewriting of the myth that attributes the infanticide to the Corinthians; see also idem, *Medea: Stimmen; Roman; Voraussetzungen zu einem Text* (Munich: Luchterhand, 2001). The literary history of the figure of Medea, from antiquity to the present, in plays, novels, and films, comprises countless versions; on this, see Davide Susanetti, *Favole antiche: Mito greco e tradizione letteraria europea* (Rome: Carocci, 2005), pp. 213–240. Another useful volume is Maria Grazia Ciani, ed., *Medea: Variazioni sul mito* (Venice: Marsilio, 2003), which assembles Italian translations of the texts of Euripides, Seneca, Grillparzer, and Alvaro.
3. Nicole Loraux, *Mothers in Mourning: With the Essay of Amnesty and Its Opposite*, trans. Corinne Pache (Ithaca, N.Y.: Cornell University Press, 1998), p. 51.
4. Susanetti, *Favole antiche*, p. 216.
5. Károly Kérenyi, *The Gods of the Greeks*, trans. Norman Cameron (London: Thames and Hudson, 1951), p. 193.

■

6. Susanetti, *Favole antiche*, pp. 215–216.
7. Euripides, *Medea*, ll. 1239–1240. Here and below, the translation is from Euripides, *Medea and Other Plays*, trans. Philip Vellacott (Harmondsworth: Penguin, 1963).
8. Ibid., l. 849.
9. Ibid., ll. 1283–1289.
10. See Davide Susanetti's ample note in his commentary on Euripides in the Italian edition of *Medea*, pp. 209–210.
11. Euripides, *Medea*, l. 1326.
12. Ibid., l. 1250.
13. Nicole Loraux, *The Experiences of Tiresias: The Feminine and the Greek Man*, trans. Paula Wissing (Princeton: Princeton University Press, 1995), p. 98.
14. Euripides, *Medea*, l. 1075.
15. W. G. Sebald, *On the Natural History of Destruction*, trans. Anthea Bell (New York: Random House, 2003), p. 27.
16. Sebald, *On the Natural History of Destruction*, p. 89.

# 7. Horrorism

1. St. Augustine, *De peccatorum meritis et remissione et de baptismo parvulorum* 1.3.
2. See Luigina Mortari, *La pratica dell'aver cura* (Milan: Mondadori, 2006).
3. This is confirmed, from a specifically Christian point of view, in a work by David Jansen, *Graced Vulnerability: A Theology of Childhood* (Cleveland: Pilgrim, 2005). In a context of theological reflection, it proposes a relational—rather than rationalistic—conception of the human being, taking the vulnerability of the infant as a paradigm.
4. See Elaine Scarry, *The Body in Pain: The Making and Unmaking of the World* (New York: Oxford University Press, 1985).
5. Corrado Bologna, "Tortura," in *Enciclopedia* (Turin: Einaudi, 1981), 14:353. [This multivolume work with a one-word title is informally but universally known to Italian readers as the "Enciclopedia Einaudi." WM]

# 8. Those Who Have Seen the Gorgon

1. Yves Ternon, *The Armenians: History of a Genocide*, trans. Rouben C. Cholakian, 2d ed. (Delmar, N.Y.: Caravan, 1990).
2. Franz V. Werfel, *The Forty Days of Musa Dagh*, trans. Geoffrey Dunlop (New York: Viking, 1934), p. 93.
3. Antonia Arslan, *La masseria delle allodole* (Milan: Rizzoli, 2004), p. 148. This novel, which reworks family experiences and memories, is accompanied by a series of essays on the Armenian genocide by the author, who has been committed for

years to keeping the historical memory of it alive, against the denialist position still taken by the present Turkish government. She has edited numerous publications for the publisher Guerini, among them Claude Metz Mutafian, *Yeghern: Breve storia del genocidio degli Armeni* (Milan: Guerini e associati, 1995); and Vahakn Dadrian, *Storia del genocidio degli Armeni* (Milan: Guerini e associati, 2003), both translations into Italian. See as well Antonia Arslan, "Metz Yeghern (il Grande Male): Memoria del male ed elaborazione del ricordo nella diaspora armena dopo il genocidio," in *La memoria del male: Percorsi tra gli stermini del Novecento e il loro ricordo*, ed. Paolo Bernardini, Diego Lucci, and Gadi Luzzato Voghera (Padua: Cleup, 2006), pp. 163–181.

4. Primo Levi, *The Drowned and the Saved*, trans. Raymond Rosenthal (New York: Summit, 1988), pp. 83–84.

5. Ibid., p. 98.

6. Jean Améry, *At the Mind's Limits: Contemplations by a Survivor on Auschwitz and Its Realities*, trans. Sidney Rosenfeld and Stella P. Rosenfeld (Bloomington: Indiana University Press, 1980), p. 9. On this, see further Wolfgang Sofsky, "The Muselmann," chap. 17 of *The Order of Terror: The Concentration Camp*, trans. William Templer (Princeton: Princeton University Press, 1997), pp. 199–205. And for an intense theoretical reading of the phenomenon of the impossible testimony of Levi, see above all Giorgio Agamben, *Remnants of Auschwitz: The Witness and the Archive*, trans. Daniel Heller-Roazen (New York: Zone, 1999), pp. 41–86.

7. Levi, *The Drowned and the Saved*, p. 84.

8. Ibid.

9. Primo Levi, If This Is a Man *and* The Truce, trans. Stuart Woolf, intro. Paul Bailey (London: Abacus, 1987), p. 96.

10. Ibid.

11. Ibid., p. 32.

12. Ibid., p. 161.

13. Levi, *The Drowned and the Saved*, p. 14.

14. "The camp was a colony of terror" (Sofsky, *The Order of Terror*, p. 14).

15. Levi, *If This Is a Man*, p. 69.

16. Levi, *The Drowned and the Saved*, p. 21.

17. Ibid., p. 111.

18. Ibid., pp. 113–114.

19. Ibid., p. 113.

20. "Sie tötete alle lebensfähigen Neugeborenen, manche durch Injektion, andere erwürgte sie oder warf sie einfach in den Wasserkübel" (Margarete Buber-Neumann, *Als Gefangene bei Stalin und Hitler* [1947; reprint, Stuttgart: Seewald, 1968], p. 222. As evinced by the title of this extraordinary piece of testimony (the German subtitle of several editions, although not of the one cited here, was *Eine Welt im Dunkel* [A world in darkness]), the author, a German communist whose first marriage was to the son of the Jewish philosopher Martin Buber, was first interned for two years in a Stalinist Lager in Karaganda and then in 1940 "consigned" to the Gestapo, which sent her to the Ravensbrück concentration camp.

[An English version is *Under Two Dictators*, trans. Edward Fitzgerald (New York: Dodd, Mead, 1949). It appears to be unreliable and silently skips over the passage quoted (see pp. 251–252), perhaps because it was thought too shocking in 1949. An Internet search in autumn 2007 indicates that a new edition is to be published by Random House in 2008, but it is not clear whether it will be a reprint of the Fitzgerald translation. WM]

21. Carlo Saletti, ed., *La voce dei sommersi* (Venice: Marsilio, 1999), p. 125.

22. The quoted passage is taken from Varlam Shalamov, *Kolyma Tales*, trans. John Glad (London: Penguin, 1994), p. 285. This work represents one of the most important testimonies to the horror of the Stalinist Lagers. Arrested during the purges of 1937 for "Trotskyist counter-revolutionary activity," Shalamov was deported to Kolyma—an ice-covered region of Siberia dotted with gold mines—where he succeeded in surviving until he was released in 1951. The lives of the detainees as described by Shalamov have many points in common with what Levi observed, among them the physical and moral degradation of the prisoners, the cruelty and arbitrariness of their jailers, the disappearance of solidarity among the internees, the hierarchy in the Lager, with the "common criminals" in a privileged position—the "grey zone"—and above all the cold and the hunger.

23. Levi, *If This Is a Man*, p. 33.

24. Levi, *The Drowned and the Saved*, p. 125.

25. "To remain clean despite all was to save a part of one's own dignity, that is, to resist," writes David Rousset, for example, in his celebrated book *Les jours de notre mort* (Paris: Pavois, 1947; reprint, Paris: Hachette, 1992), 2:212.

26. Levi, *If This Is a Man*, p. 93.

27. Ibid., p. 48.

28. Levi, *The Drowned and the Saved*, p. 38.

29. Levi, *If This Is a Man*, p. 80.

30. Levi, *The Truce*, p. 188.

31. Ibid., p. 188.

32. Agamben, *Remnants of Auschwitz*, p. 104.

33. Agamben, *Remnants of Auschwitz*, p. 106.

34. Levi, *The Drowned and the Saved*, p. 53.

35. Ibid., pp. 48–49.

## 9. Auschwitz; or, On Extreme Horror

1. Hannah Arendt, *The Origins of Totalitarianism* (1951; new ed., New York: Harcourt, Brace and World, 1966), p. 456.

2. Ibid., pp. 458–459.

3. Ibid., p. 459.

4. See Simona Forti's introduction to the collection edited by her, *La filosofia di fronte all'estremo* (Turin: Einaudi, 2004), p. xvii.

5. Hannah Arendt, "Mankind and Terror," in *Essays in Understanding, 1930–1954*, ed. Jerome Kohn (New York: Harcourt, Brace, 1994), p. 297.

6. Arendt, *The Origins of Totalitarianism*, p. 440.

7. Ibid.

8. Ibid., p. xxx, from the preface to the first edition, dated 1950. On this, see Olivia Guaraldo, *Storylines. Politics, History and Narrative from an Arendtian Perspective* (Jyväskylä, Finland: SoPhi, 2001), pp. 132ff.

9. Ibid., p. 440.

10. Ibid., p. 444.

11. Philosophers writing in Italian are particularly interesting and theoretically fertile in this respect; I limit myself to noting Giorgio Agamben, *Homo Sacer: Sovereign Power and Bare Life*, trans. Daniel Heller-Roazen (Stanford, Calif.: Stanford University Press, 1998); Roberto Esposito, *Bios* (Turin: Einaudi, 2004); Laura Bazzicalupo, *Il governo delle vite* (Rome: Laterza, 2006); the authors of the various essays contained in *Filosofia politica*, no. 3 (2003) and no. 1 (2006), especially Simona Forti, "Biopolitica delle anime," pp. 397–417 in the former, for its original take on the relationship between biopolitics and totalitarianism; and finally the authors of the essays in *Biopolitica: Storia e attualità di un concetto* (Verona: Ombre corte, 2003). As for Michel Foucault, the seminal text is still *"Society Must Be Defended": Lectures at the Collège de France, 1975—1976*, ed. Mauro Bertani and Alessandro Fontana, gen. ed. François Ewald and Alessandro Fontana, trans. David Macey (New York: Picador, 2003); to it should be added, at least, *Security, Territory, Population: Lectures at the Collège de France, 1977–1978*, ed. Michel Senellart; gen. ed. François Ewald and Alessandro Fontana, trans. Graham Burchell (New York: Palgrave Macmillan, 2007); and *Naissance de la biopolitique: Cours au Collège de France (1978–1979)*, ed. Michel Senellart, gen. ed. François Ewald and Alessandro Fontana (Paris: Gallimard/Seuil, 2004).

12. Arendt, *The Origins of Totalitarianism*, p. 457.

13. Ibid., p. 454.

14. Ibid., p. 443.

15. Ibid., p. 453.

16. Ibid.

17. Ibid., p. 455.

18. Ibid.

19. Hannah Arendt, *The Human Condition* (1958), 2d ed., intro. Margaret Canovan (Chicago: University of Chicago Press, 1998).

20. Arendt, *The Origins of Totalitarianism*, pp. 453, 454.

21. Simona Forti, *Vita della mente e tempo della polis* (Milan: Franco Angeli, 1996), p. 177; emphasis added.

22. Arendt, *The Origins of Totalitarianism*, p. 457.

23. Hannah Arendt and Karl Jaspers, *Correspondence, 1926–1969*, ed. Lotte Kohler and Hans Saner, trans. Robert Kimber and Rita Kimber (New York: Harcourt Brace Jovanovich, 1992), letter no. 109, 4 March 1951, pp. 165–168; the quotations are from p. 166.

24. Ibid.

25. Simona Forti analyzes this theme masterfully in *Vita della mente*, pp. 91–204. See also my article "Politicizing Theory," *Political Theory* 4 (2002): 506–531.

26. Tzvetan Todorov, *Hope and Memory: Lessons from the Twentieth Century*, trans. David Bellos (Princeton: Princeton University Press, 2003), p. 3.

27. As indicated by the famous subtitle of her book on the Eichmann trial, *Eichmann in Jerusalem: A Report on the Banality of Evil* (1963), rev. ed. (New York: Penguin, 1977, 1994), Arendt's thinking about evil continued to develop and deepen after the book on totalitarianism. In the critical literature on Arendt, this is one of the most debated topics; see especially Simona Forti, "Banalità del male," in *I concetti del male*, ed. Pier Paolo Portinaro (Turin: Einaudi, 2002), pp. 30–52; and Forti's essay "Le figure del male," which prefaces the Italian translation of *The Origins of Totalitarianism*, *Le origini del totalitarismo* (Turin: Edizioni di comunità, 1999). For a treatment of the topic with strongly Arendtian accents, see Richard Bernstein, *Radical Evil* (Cambridge: Polity, 2002). Many contemporary texts on the question of evil discuss Arendt's thesis and the problems she raises, among them, Michele Nicoletti, *La politica e il male* (Brescia: Morcelliana, 2000); Susan Neiman, *Evil in Modern Thought* (Princeton: Princeton University Press, 2002); María Pía Lara, ed., *Rethinking Evil: Contemporary Perspectives* (Berkeley: University of California Press, 2001); Adam Morton, *On Evil* (New York: Routledge, 2004); Rüdiger Safranski, *Das Böse; oder, Das Drama der Freiheit* (Munich: Hanser, 1997).

# 10. Erotic Carnages

1. Hannah Arendt, *The Origins of Totalitarianism* (1951; new ed., New York: Harcourt, Brace and World, 1966), p. 439 n. 126. See David Rousset, *Les jours de notre mort* (Paris: Pavois, 1947; reprint, Paris: Hachette, 1992). Arendt's positive judgment also extended to Rousset's *L'univers concentrationnaire* (Paris: Pavois, 1946). That work was rapidly published in English as *The Other Kingdom*, trans. Ramon Guthrie (New York: Reynal and Hitchcock, 1947), a copy of which Arendt sent to Hermann Broch—confirmation that Arendt was greatly interested in Rousset. See Arendt's letter to Broch dated 30 December 1948, no. 34, pp. 89–90, in Hannah Arendt and Herman Broch, *Briefwechsel: 1946 bis 1951*, ed. Paul Michael Lützeler (Frankfurt: Jüdischer Verlag, 1996).

2. Arendt, *The Origins of Totalitarianism*, p. 437.

3. Ibid., p. 441.

4. Tzvetan Todorov, "The Achievement of David Rousset," in *Hope and Memory: Lessons from the Twentieth Century*, trans. David Bellos (Princeton: Princeton University Press, 2003), pp. 148–158; see especially pp. 157–158.

5. Arendt, *The Origins of Totalitarianism*, p. 441. To this passage is attached her n. 131, which states: "See Georges Bataille in *Critique*, January, 1948, p. 72." Bataille's

review of Rousset, entitled "Refléxions sur le bourreau et la victime," appeared in *Critique* 17 (October 1947): 337–342 (it is now available in Georges Bataille, *Oeuvres complètes*, 12 vols. [Paris: Gallimard, 1970–1988], 11:262–267). Arendt evidently cites the wrong issue of *Critique*. More than that, she seems to misinterpret Bataille's words. He writes: "what can precisely be admired in the fact of the trial overcome, and in the victory of life, is that, finding itself in the power of horror, and knowing itself to be at the mercy of physical misery, life nevertheless *is certain* that, through an excess of firmness over sordid filth, it will prevail overall" ("Et ce qui peut précisément être admiré dans le fait de l'épreuve surmontée et dans la victoire de la vie, c'est que, se découvrant dans le pouvoir de l'horreur et se sachant à la merci de la misère physique, la vie *s'assure* néanmoins que, par un excès de la fermeté sur l'immondice, elle l'emportera dans l'ensemble"; Bataille, *Oeuvres complètes*, 11:264). If it is in fact acceptable to interpret "fermeté sur l'immondice" as "dwelling on horrors," there is very little in Bataille's text to justify the accusation that he thinks it "superficial" to "dwell on horrors"— unless Arendt means here to suggest that Bataille is accusing Rousset of not going all the way in recognizing that "the depth of the horror of things proposes itself to the human being as the truth to discover" ("le fond d'horreur des choses se propose à l'être humain comme la vérité à découvrir"; ibid.). This last is indeed a genuinely Bataillean thesis, but in the review it is not directed against any putative "superficiality" on Rousset's part. As for Arendt's mistake about the date, it is worth mentioning that the October 1946 issue of *Critique* had published a review by Charles Autrand of *L'univers concentrationnaire* (pp. 441–447), but Autrand says nothing about dwelling on horrors.

6. Arendt, *The Origins of Totalitarianism*, p. 330 n. 56. She refers readers to Georges Bataille, "Le secret de Sade," *Critique* 3, nos. 15–16 and 17 (1947). Bataille's essays were subsequently reprinted in Georges Bataille, *La littérature et le mal* (Paris: Gallimard, 1957), which in turn is incorporated in *Oeuvres complètes*, vol. 6; the essays appear in the section entitled "Sade" at pp. 239–257. [For all the author's references to various works of Georges Bataille, I supply references and quotations from *Oeuvres complètes*, with my own translations from the French. WM]

7. Bataille, *La littérature et le mal*, in *Oeuvres complètes*, 6:250.

8. Bataille, *La littérature et le mal*, in *Oeuvres complètes*, 6:255, 253 (emphasis in the original).

9. Bataille, *La littérature et le mal*, in *Oeuvres complètes*, 6:254.

10. Arendt quotes the phrase "looking for the sublime in the infamous" in *The Origins of Totalitarianism*, p. 330 n. 56; it is from an introduction by Jean Paulhan to an edition of one of Sade's works, published in 1946.

11. Arendt, *The Origins of Totalitarianism*, pp. 330, 331.

12. Ibid., p. 327.

13. Ibid., p. 49, where Arendt signals the "simple thesis, ingenious . . ." elaborated by Céline in *Bagatelle pour un massacre* (1937) and *École des cadavres* (1938). (Arendt errs, however, in giving 1938 as the year of publication of *Bagatelle pour un massacre*.)

14. Louis-Ferdinand Céline, *Voyage au bout de la nuit* (Paris: Gallimard, 1952): "On faisait queue pour aller crever" (p. 30); "tout s'est rétréci au meurtre" (p. 40); "au cimetière ardent des batailles" (p. 50); "saucissons de bataille" (p. 68); "le grand écartelage" (p. 64). [My translation, here and below. W.M.]

15. In *La critique sociale* 7 (1933), reprinted in *Oeuvres complètes*, 1:321–322.

16. Céline, *Voyage au bout de la nuit*, p. 337.

17. Alain Badiou, *The Century*, trans. Alberto Toscana (Cambridge: Polity, 2007), p. 123.

18. Arendt, *The Origins of Totalitarianism*, p. 328.

19. Bataille, *La littérature et le mal*, in *Oeuvres complètes*, 6:255.

20. Georges Bataille, Pierre Klossowski, Jean Hyppolite, Jean-Paul Sartre, et al., "Discussion sur le péché," annex 5 in Bataille, *Oeuvres complètes*, 6:315–359; the speaker is Bataille in the passage quoted, at p. 342. (This "debate on sin" is the transcription of a public event held in Paris in 1944).

21. Georges Bataille, "Hegel, la mort, et le sacrifice," in *Oeuvres complètes*, 12:337.

22. On this, and on the crucial relation of Bataille to Hegel, see Jacques Derrida's essay "From Restricted to General Economy: A Hegelianism Without Reserve," chap. 9 in *Writing and Difference*, trans. and ed. Alan Bass (1978; reprint, London: Routledge, 2001), pp. 317–350.

23. On the relations between Bataille and Kojève and on Bataille's writings on Nietzsche, see Roberto Esposito, *Categorie dell'impolitico* (Bologna: Il Mulino, 1988), pp. 263ff.

24. Elena Pulcini, "Il bisogno di *dépense*: Pulsioni, sacro, sovranità in G. Bataille," *Filosofia politica* 1 (1994): 99; emphasis in the original.

25. Jean-Luc Nancy, *The Inoperative Community*, trans. Peter Connor, Lisa Garbus, Michael Holland, and Simona Sawhney, ed. Peter Connor (Minneapolis: University of Minnesota Press, 1991), p. 17.

26. Georges Bataille, *L'érotisme*, in *Oeuvres complètes*, 10:22.

27. Ibid., 10:25.

28. Ibid., 10:186.

29. Bataille et al., "Discussion sur le péché," in Bataille, *Oeuvres complètes*, 6:358.

30. Nancy, *The Inoperative Community*, p. 34.

31. Bataille, *Sur Nietzsche*, in *Oeuvres complètes*, 6:45.

32. Esposito, *Categorie dell'impolitico*, p. 300.

33. Ibid., p. 304.

34. Nancy, *The Inoperative Community*, p. 35.

## 11. So Mutilated that It Might Be the Body of a Pig

1. Susan Sontag, *Regarding the Pain of Others* (New York: Farrar, Straus and Giroux, 2003), p. 116.

2. Virginia Woolf, *Three Guineas* (New York: Harcourt, Brace, 1938), pp. 14–15.

3. Sontag, *Regarding the Pain*, p. 109.
4. Ibid., p. 98. Sontag had already addressed Bataille's taste for pornography in an essay that appears in the English edition of Bataille's *Story of the Eye* (London: Penguin, 1982), pp. 83–118.
5. *Les larmes d'Éros* appears in Georges Bataille, *Oeuvres complètes*, 12 vols. (Paris: Gallimard, 1970–1988), 10:573–625.
6. Sontag, *Regarding the Pain*, p. 99.
7. Bataille, *Les larmes d'Éros*, in *Oeuvres complètes*, 10:626.
8. Ibid., 10:619.
9. *Le procès de Gilles de Rais* appears in Bataille, *Oeuvres complètes*, vol. 10.
10. Bataille, *Les larmes d'Éros*, in *Oeuvres complètes*, 10:627.
11. Sontag, *Regarding the Pain*, p. 95.
12. Ibid. p. 41.
13. Ibid. p. 98.
14. Ibid. p. 97.
15. Jacqueline Rose, "Deadly Embrace," *London Review of Books*, 4 November 2004.
16. This is the English text as it appears on the Internet at www.imra.org.il/story.php3?id=13385. I should point out that the context is a very critical discussion, bordering on the offensively aggressive, of Spivak's paper of 22 June 2002, which was entitled *Translating Class, Altering Hospitality*. The passage cited subsequently appeared in slightly different form in print in Gayatri Chakravorty Spivak, "Terror: A Speech After 9–11," *boundary 2* 31, no. 2 (2004): 81–111.
17. Pierre Klossowski, from his introduction to the ideas of Georges Bataille in Georges Bataille, Pierre Klossowski, Jean Hyppolite, Jean-Paul Sartre, et al., "Discussion sur le péché," in Bataille, *Oeuvres complètes*, 6:318. The quotations in the text are from this page and p. 317.

## 12. The Warrior's Pleasure

1. Marcello Flores, *Tutta la violenza di un secolo* (Milan: Feltrinelli, 2005), p. 68.
2. Ibid., p. 12
3. See Pier Paolo Portinaro, "Genocidio," in *I concetti del male*, ed. Pier Paolo Portinaro (Turin: Einaudi, 2002), pp. 104–117.
4. Varlam Salamov, *I racconti della Kolyma*, trans. Marco Binni (Milan: Adelphi, 1995), p. 329. [The quotation has been translated from the Italian; this passage is not found in the English translation of Shalamov's *Kolyma Tales*. WM]
5. "Induced famines" are reported in the case of the social experiments in connection with the "great leap forward" in China (1958–1962), which had their atrocious precedent in the Ukraine, which was reduced to starvation by the Stalinist regime (winter 1932–1933).
6. W. G. Sebald, *On the Natural History of Destruction*, trans. Anthea Bell (New York: Random House, 2003), p. 19.

7. Flores, *Tutta la violenza*, pp. 57, 172.

8. The source of this figure is a study by a group of researchers from the Johns Hopkins Bloomberg School of Public Health, published on the Internet site of the journal *The Lancet* on 11 October 2006.

9. Alain Badiou, *The Century*, trans. Alberto Toscana (Cambridge: Polity, 2007), p. 26. On mass violence, in particular genocide and war crimes in the global era, with reference as well to the problem of the "census of the victims," see Maria Calloni, ed., *Violenza senza legge* (Turin: UTET, 2006).

10. Giovanni De Luna, *Il corpo del nemico ucciso* (Turin: Einaudi, 2006), p. xviii.

11. John Collins and Ross Glover, eds., introduction to *Collateral Language: A User's Guide to America's New War* (New York: New York University Press, 2002), p. 8.

12. Hannah Arendt, "On Violence," in *Crises of the Republic: Lying in Politics, Civil Disobedience, On Violence, Thoughts on Politics, and Revolution* (New York: Harcourt, Brace, Jovanovich, 1972), pp. 157–158.

13. Ibid., p. 107.

14. Sigmund Freud, "The Ego and the Id" (1923), in *The Standard Edition of the Complete Psychological Works of Sigmund Freud*, trans. James Strachey et al. (London: Hogarth, 1955–), 19:40.

15. Ibid., 19:41.

16. James Hillman, *A Terrible Love Of War* (New York: Penguin, 2004), p. 214.

17. Ibid., chap. 3, pp. 104ff. Burke should also be mentioned, whose celebrated thesis on terror and horror as sources of the sublime obviously deserve full and ramified discussion, which I do not undertake here. Apart from recalling that this thesis was fundamental for the definite entry of the concepts of terror and horror into the field of aesthetics, I limit myself to noting that, symptomatically, terror and horror are coupled without the author's insisting particularly on the distinction between them. See Edmund Burke, *A Philosophical Enquiry into the Origin of Our Ideas of the Sublime and Beautiful*, ed. Adam Phillips (New York: Oxford University Press, 1998).

18. Ibid., p. 214.

19. Ibid., p. 106.

20. Ibid., p. 110.

21. Ibid., p. 1, 55, 142.

22. René Girard, chap. 5 in *Violence and the Sacred*, trans. Patrick Gregory (Baltimore: Johns Hopkins University Press, 1977), p. 124.

23. De Luna, *Il corpo del nemico ucciso*, p. xiv.

## 13. Worldwide Aggressiveness

1. Carl Schmitt, *Un giurista davanti a se stesso* (Vicenza: Neri Pozza, 2005), p. 38. [The passage in the text is my translation into English of the Italian translation cited by the author, which is an original anthology of writings by Schmitt not oth-

erwise available to me. It comes from a lecture published as "El orden del mundo después de la segunda guerra mundial," *Revista de estudios politicos* 122 (1962): 19–36.]

2. Carl von Clausewitz, *On War*, trans. and ed. Michael Howard and Peter Paret (1976), rev. ed. (Princeton: Princeton University Press, 1984).

3. Carl Schmitt, *Theory of the Partisan*, trans. A. C. Goodson, *New Centennial Review*, p. 32, msupress.msu.edu/journals/cr/schmitt.pdf (accessed 2008). [The editors of the Internet journal that published this work state: "The New Centennial Review is proud to present a complete translation of Carl Schmitt's *Theory of the Partisan* in conjunction with CR Volume 4 Number 3." The title of the original work, published in 1963, is *Theorie des Partisanen: Zwischenbemerkung zum Begriff des Politischen*. Cavarero cites the Italian translation, *Teoria del partigiano* (Milan: Il Saggiatore, 1981). WM]

4. Ibid., p. 26.

5. Ibid., p. 6.

6. See Carl Schmitt, *The Concept of the Political*, expanded ed., trans. and ed. George Schwab, foreword Tracy B. Strong (Chicago: University of Chicago Press, 2007).

7. Carlo Galli, *Genealogia della politica: Carl Schmitt e la crisi del pensiero politico moderno* (Bologna: Il Mulino, 1996), p. 766.

8. Ibid.

9. Schmitt, *Theory of the Partisan*, p. 26.

10. Galli, *Genealogia della politica*, p. 767.

11. On p. 52 of *Theory of the Partisan*, Schmitt speaks of "world-aggressive purposes" and "world-revolutionary aggression."

12. On this, I refer to Lee Salter, "Problems of Politics, Media, and Truth: The BBC's Representation of the Invasion of Iraq," *Critical Studies in Mass Communication*, forthcoming.

13. On the problems of naming violence today and the political aspects of such naming, I refer once more to the essays collected in John Collins and Ross Glover, eds., *Collateral Language: A User's Guide to America's New War* (New York: New York University Press, 2002).

14. Schmitt, *Theory of the Partisan*, p. 42.

15. Karl Marx and Friedrich Engels, *The Holy Family*, in *Marx/Engels Collected Works* (New York: International Publishers, 1975–2005), 4:123; emphasis in the original.

16. Schmitt, *Theory of the Partisan*, p. 66.

17. Ibid., p. 67.

18. Ibid.

19. Hannah Arendt, *The Origins of Totalitarianism* (1951), new ed. (New York: Harcourt, Brace and World, 1966), p. 424.

20. Giacomo Marramao, *Passagio a Occidente* (Turin: Bollati Boringhieri, 2003), p. 123.

21. Charles Townshend, *Terrorism: A Very Short Introduction* (Oxford: Oxford University Press, 2002).

22. Ibid., p. 3

23. Clausewitz, *On War*, 1.4, p. 77.

24. Townshend, *Terrorism*, p. 8.

25. Michael Walzer, *Arguing About War* (New Haven: Yale University Press, 2005), p. 130.

26. Schmitt, *Theory of the Partisan*, p. 20.

27. I use the extracts from the sentence published in the article by Luigi Ferrarella and Giuseppe Guastella in *Corriere della Sera*, 19 July 2005.

28. Collins and Glover, introduction to *Collateral Language*, p. 7.

29. Marramao, *Passagio a Occidente*, p. 44.

30. Arjun Appadurai, *Fear of Small Numbers* (Durham, N.C.: Duke University Press, 2006), p. 92.

31. See Walzer, *Arguing About War*, in which, in light of the "war on terror," he updates the views presented in his now-classic work, *Just and Unjust Wars* (New York: Basic Books, 1977).

32. Thomas Nagel, "War and Massacre," *Philosophy and Public Affairs* 1, no. 2 (1972): 127.

33. Carlo Galli, *La guerra globale* (Rome: Laterza, 2002), p. 64.

34. Appadurai, *Fear of Small Numbers*, p. 31.

35. Ibid., pp. 31–32.

36. Khaled Fouad Allam, *Lettera a un kamikaze* (Milan: Rizzoli, 2004), p. 15.

37. Angelo Bolaffi and Giacomo Marramao, *Frammento e sistema* (Rome: Donzelli, 2001), p. 166.

## 14. For a History of Terror

1. Charles Townshend, *Terrorism: A Very Short Introduction* (Oxford: Oxford University Press, 20), p. 36.

2. Remo Bodei, "Ragione e terrore: Sulla tirannide giacobina della virtù," *Il centauro* 3 (1981): 42, 43.

3. Hannah Arendt, "On Revolution," in *Crises of the Republic: Lying in Politics, Civil Disobedience, On Violence, Thoughts on Politics, and Revolution* (New York: Harcourt, Brace, Jovanovich, 1972), p. 95. On this, see further Arno J. Mayer, *The Furies: Violence and Terror in the French and Russian Revolutions* (Princeton: Princeton University Press, 2000).

4. Thomas Hobbes, *Leviathan*, ed. C. B. MacPherson (New York: Penguin, 1968), pt. 1, chap. 11, p. 161.

5. Hobbes, *Leviathan*, pt. 2, chap. 17, p. 227.

6. Hobbes, *Leviathan*, pt. 2, chap. 17, p. 223. The same chapter also supplies confirmation of the need for terror to guarantee security: "For by this Authoritie, given him by every particular man in the Common-Wealth, he hath the use of so much Power and Strength conferred on him, that by terror thereof, he is inabled to forme the wills of them all, to Peace at home, and mutuall ayd against their enemies abroad" (pp. 227–228).

7. In the lecture *Politik als Beruf*; see Max Weber, *The Vocation Lectures*, trans. Rodney Livingstone, ed. David Owen and Tracy B. Strong (Indianapolis: Hackett, 2004).

8. Starting from a comparison of Hobbes and Montesquieu, the theme is developed in Corey Robin, *Fear: The History of a Political Idea* (New York: Oxford University Press, 2004).

9. Townshend, *Terrorism*, p. 5.

10. John Collins, "Terrorism," in *Collateral Language: A User's Guide to America's New War*, ed. John Collins and Ross Glover (New York: New York University Press, 2002), p. 155.

11. Giovanni Sartori, "Illusionisti pericolosi," *Corriere della Sera*, 24 July 2005 (written right after the bombings at Sharm el Sheikh that caused more than one hundred deaths).

12. Jessica Stern, *Terror in the Name of God* (New York: HarperCollins, 2003), p. xx. See also the section "The Rhetoric of Terrorism" in chap. 6, "The Political Uses of Massacre and Genocide," in Jacques Sémelin, *Purify and Destroy: The Political Uses of Massacre and Genocide*, trans. Cynthia Schoch (New York: Columbia University Press, 2007), pp. 348–361; Sémelin reviews the acceptations of the term "terrorism" in the course of his study of massacre, genocide, and the "process of destruction."

13. Luigi Bonante, "Terrorismo politico," in *Dizionario di politica*, ed. Norberto Bobbio, Nicola Matteucci, and Gianfranco Pasquino (Turin: UTET, 2004), pp. 980–981.

14. Danilo Zolo, "Le ragioni del 'terrorismo globale,'" *Iride* 46 (2005): 485. Zolo denounces such a principle as "a gaping lacuna in the international order."

15. Arjun Appadurai, *Fear of Small Numbers* (Durham, N.C.: Duke University Press, 2006), p. 2.

16. Ibid., p. 12. Insisting in many speeches after September 11 that "the American way of life is non-negotiable," President George W. Bush evidently meant to respond to this threat. As regards the modernity that is under attack today by Al-Qaeda, not only is it a synonym of the West, it is substantially reducible to such categories as individualism, capitalism, materialism, imperialism, and above all secularization. As the reader will notice, these are all categories internal to the historical development of the modern state, but which are subsumed here within the stereotype of a lifestyle whose moral depravity and irreligiosity are emphasized.

17. The expression is Alberto Toscano's, drawn from "Il fanatismo, da Lutero a Bin Laden," *Reset* 97 (2006): 32. The same issue of this journal contains a useful brief glossary compiled by Sadik J. Al-Azm, "Il pericolo dell'islamismo" (p. 31).

18. Mark Juergensmeyer, *Terror in the Mind of God: The Global Rise of Religious Violence* (2000), 3d ed. (Berkeley: University of California Press, 2003), p. 217. The title of the Italian translation is *Terroristi in nome di Dio* (Rome: Laterza, 2003), which actually is a literal translation of the title of a different book, cited above, Jessica Stern's *Terror in the Name of God*. The latter is worth mentioning again in this connection, and not just because of the aptness of its title. She is also the author of *The Ultimate Terrorists* (Cambridge: Harvard University Press, 1999).

■

19. See José Sanmartin, "Sentieri Jihadisti," *Intelligence* 1 (2005): 36.

20. Appadurai, *Fear of Small Numbers*, p. 111.

21. On the complexity of the category "fundamentalism" and its abuse by the media, see the studies of Renzo Guolo, *Il fondamentalismo islamico* (Rome: Laterza, 2002) and, more recently, *Il partito di Dio: L'Islam radicale contro l'Occidente* (Milan: Guerrini, 2005), as well as the volume cowritten with Enzo Pace, *I fondamentalismi* (Rome: Laterza, 2002).

22. Gilles Kepel, introduction to *Al-Qaida dans le texte: Écrits d'Oussama ben Laden, Abdallah Azzam, Ayman al-Zawahiri et Abou Moussab al-Zarqawi*, ed. Gilles Kepel et al. (Paris: PUF, 2005), p. 4.

23. Robespierre, speech of 28 pluviôse, year II.

24. Though they do not embrace the classic thesis of Franz Fanon concerning the violence of the oppressed as a purifying force with the power to redeem them from humiliation and restore their dignity, the large majority of contemporary analyses of terrorism highlight humiliation as an important factor. See, for example, Bernard Lewis, *What Went Wrong? The Clash Between Islam and Modernity in the Middle East* (New York: Oxford University Press, 2002), which broaches themes taken up subsequently in his *Crisis of Islam: Holy War and Unholy Terror* (New York: Modern Library, 2003).

25. I refer once more to the analysis presented in Appadurai, *Fear of Small Numbers*, pp. 17 passim.

26. Ernst Jünger, *Der Waldgang* (Frankfurt: Vittorio Klostermann, 1951), p. 78. [The translations from the German are my own. The author cites the Italian translation, *Trattato del ribelle* (Milan: Adelphi, 2004). WM]

27. Ibid., p. 85.

28. Ibid., pp. 50 and 79.

29. Jünger deals specifically with the theme of crossing the "line" of nihilism in a well-known essay of 1950, written on the occasion of the sixtieth birthday of Martin Heidegger, to which Heidegger responded. See Ernst Jünger, *Über die Linie* (Frankfurt: Vittorio Klostermann, 1950); and Martin Heidegger, *The Question of Being*, trans. William Kluback and Jean T. Wilde (New York: Twayne, 1958). See further Franco Volpi, *Il nichilismo* (Rome: Laterza, 1996), pp. 69–78, and Franca D'Agostini, *Logica nel nichilismo* (Rome: Laterza, 2000), pp. 269ff.

30. Jünger, *Der Waldgang*, p. 137.

31. Ibid., sec. 31, pp. 122ff.

32. Ibid., p. 136.

33. Ibid., p. 80.

## 15. Suicidal Horrorism

1. Actually, Kamikaze was the name of the most famous unit of the "special attack squadrons," called *tokubetsu kohgeki tai*, abbreviated as *tokko*.

2. I have made the (possibly debatable) choice to use the masculine singular "*shahid*" to include both the plural "*shuhada*" or the feminine "*shahida*." The latter is

a neologism in Arabic; apparently it was first used by Yasser Arafat in a speech in 2002.

3. Leonardo Sacco, *Kamikaze e Shahid* (Rome: Bulzoni, 2005), p. 25.

4. Ibid., p. 157.

5. See Christopher Reuter, *My Life Is a Weapon: A Modern History of Suicide Bombing* (Princeton: Princeton University Press, 2004), p. 17.

6. Ibid., pp. 42ff.

7. Sacco, *Kamikaze e Shahid*, p. 166. See also Reuter, *My Life Is a Weapon*, pp. 65–78.

8. As proof of how interesting the incorrect way the Italian language still designates Islamic suicide bombers is, it is worth emphasizing that they actually do have a link with the kamikaze. The members of the terrorist group who attacked Tel Aviv airport on 30 May 1972, spreading panic and death among the crowd, were Japanese and were influenced by "the spirit of the Japanese kamikaze" (Sacco, *Kamikaze e Shahid*, p. 101).

9. Here I obviously allude to the celebrated work of Edward W. Said, *Orientalism* (1978; reprint, New York: Vintage, 1994).

10. See Ernst H. Kantorowicz, "*Pro Patria Mori* in Medieval Political Thought," in *Selected Studies* (Locust Valley, N.Y.: J. J. Augustin, 1965), pp. 308–324. Kantorowicz emphasizes the relation between patriotic martyrs and the tradition of Christian martyrdom, which had its culmination in the crusades to the Holy Land. As he notes, the venerable forebear Cacciaguida, who died fighting in the Second Crusade and now resides in paradise, says to Dante: "And I came from martyrdom to this peace" (*Paradiso, The Divine Comedy*, 15.148). As for Christian martyrdom, addressing the topic here would lead me too far afield. In this case, the function of the body of the martyr, the true residual testimony (*reliquia*) of his "act," is principally a posthumous function that serves to "colonize space and time," the *bios*, with the help of *zoe aionios*; see Stefano Salzani, "La città dci martiri: Bios e zoe aionios," *Teologia politica* 3 (2007).

11. See Rosella Prezzo, "Il corpo pornografico del guerriero," *aut-aut* 330 (2006): 13–28.

12. On this, I take the liberty of referring to my own *Stately Bodies: Literature, Philosophy, and the Question of Gender*, trans. Robert de Lucca and Deanna Shemek (Ann Arbor: University of Michigan Press, 2002), originally published as *Corpo in figure* (Milan: Feltrinelli, 1995). [The author refers to the celebrated *comité de salut public* of the French Revolution. This title is rendered in Italian as *comitato di salute pubblica*, which literally means "committee of public health," so the links she posits with the metaphor of the body politic is unproblematic in Italian. In modern French, however, the word for "health" is "*santé*," and the word "*salut*" means "safety" or "salvation." The standard English translation for the committee in question is "committee of public safety." In a private communication in 2008, the author points to the common etymology of the French "*salut*" (m.) and the Italian "*salute*" (f.) from the Latin "*salus*" (f.), which means both "health" and "safety." WM]

13. Carlo Galli, *La guerra globale* (Rome: Laterza, 2002), p. 63; Giovanni De Luna, *Il corpo del nemico ucciso* (Turin: Einaudi, 2006), pp. 36ff.

14. Stefanella Campana and Carla Reschia, *Quando l'orrore è donna* (Rome: Editori Riuniti, 2005), p. 55.
15. Stefano Salzani, "Teologia politica islamica: Un approccio," in *Teologie politiche islamiche*, ed. Stefano Salzani (Genoa: Marietti, 2006), p. 45.
16. See Ronald Jones, "Orrore e ritualità," *Intelligence* 1 (2005): 120.
17. According to the study of Robert A. Pape, *Dying to Win* (New York: Random House, 2006), the number of suicide attacks from 1980 to 2003 is a little more than three hundred.

## 16. When the Bomb Is a Woman's Body

1. See Noa Bonetti, *Io, donna kamikaze* (Rome: Iris, 2005), p. 42.
2. Ibid., pp. 101–102.
3. Julija Juzik, *Le fidanzate di Allah* (Rome: Manifestolibri, 2004). The book includes photographs in which horror is accompanied by an inevitable pity for the young faces of the suicide bombers. [See chap. 2, n. 3, above. Translations into English here are made from this Italian translation of the Russian original. WM]
4. Ibid., p. 15.
5. See Roberta Freudiani, introduction to ibid., p. 9. She in turn refers to Carlo Gubitosa, *Viaggio in Cecenia* (Nuova Iniziativa Editoriale), a publication distributed with the daily newspaper *L'Unità* in March 2004, pp. 25–43.
6. Barbara Victor, *Army of Roses: Inside the World of Palestinian Women Suicide Bombers*, foreword Christopher Dickey (Emmaus, Pa.: Rodale, 2003), p. 7.
7. Stefanella Campana and Carla Reschia, *Quando l'orrore è donna* (Rome: Editori Riuniti, 2005), p. 57.
8. Anselma dell'Olio, preface to Bonetti, *Io, donna kamikaze*, p. 7.
9. For the story related here, I depend on the account given in Victor, *Army of Roses*, pp. 222–232, from which the quoted passages below are taken. See as well Bonetti, *Io, donna kamikaze*, pp. 29–35.

## 17. Female Torturers Grinning at the Camera

1. Michel Foucault, *Discipline and Punish: The Birth of the Prison*, trans. Alan Sheridan (London: Penguin, 1977), p. 11.
2. Ibid., pp. 33–34.
3. Ibid., p. 48.
4. Ibid., p. 49.
5. Ibid., p. 35.
6. See Alessandro Pastore, *Le regole dei corpi* (Bologna: Il Mulino, 2006), pp. 101–124, in which he develops a very interesting Foucauldian analysis of the medical aspects of torture in the seventeenth and eighteenth centuries.
7. Foucault, *Discipline and Punish*, p. 49.
8. Ibid., pp. 51, 55.

9. Ibid., p. 40.

10. The best-known defender of this view is the American criminal lawyer Alan M. Dershowitz, a member of the Harvard law faculty. See, for example, his book *Why Terrorism Works: Understanding the Threat and Responding to the Challenge* (New Haven: Yale University Press, 2002), in which chapter 4 is entitled "Should the Ticking Bomb Terrorist Be Tortured? A Case Study in How a Democracy Should Make Tragic Choices."

11. Stefanella Campana and Carla Reschia, *Quando l'orrore è donna* (Rome: Editori Riuniti, 2005), p. 42.

12. Judith Butler writes acutely about the reanimation of sovereignty in the chapter of *Precarious Life* entitled "Indefinite Detention," referring to the treatment of the prisoners held in detention at Guantánamo. Her thesis, elaborated with reference to Foucault's reflections on governmentality, is that these illegal and violent practices are connected to "a ghostly and forceful resurgence of sovereignty in the midst of governmentality" (*Precarious Life: The Powers of Mourning and Violence* [London: Verso, 2004], p. 59). [Cavarero uses the Italian words "*spettro*" and "*spettralità*" often in these essays; I use "specter" and "spectrality" to translate them. But they could also be translated "ghost" and "ghostliness," as shown in reverse in this quoted phrase, where Judith Butler writes "ghostly" in English, and the Italian translation of her book used by Cavarero, *Vite precarie*, translates it by "*spettrale*." WM] I take the view that, in the Abu Ghraib affair—which came to light after Butler had written the essay in question—spectrality, especially in the forms of phantasm, mimesis, and simulation, is indeed a decisive aspect. I also owe to her celebrated book *Gender Trouble* (New York: Routledge, 1990) the category of parody, although I use it with a different and entirely negative meaning.

13. Reported by Campana and Reschia, *Quando l'orrore è donna*, p. 46.

14. Hannah Arendt, "Lying in Politics," in *Crises of the Republic: Lying in Politics, Civil Disobedience, On Violence, Thoughts on Politics, and Revolution* (New York: Harcourt, Brace, Jovanovich, 1972). In the Italian translation, *La menzogna in politica* (Genoa: Marietti, 2006), see especially the introductory essay by Olivia Guaraldo, "Le verità della politica," pp. vii–xxviii.

15. Elaine Scarry, *The Body in Pain: The Making and Unmaking of the World* (New York: Oxford University Press, 1985), p. 27.

16. The expression appears in an editorial in the journal *Leggendaria*, edited by Anna Maria Crispino, in a special issue, no. 45 (June 2004), dedicated to the torture at Abu Ghraib.

17. See Campana and Reschia, *Quando l'orrore è donna*, p. 168.

18. Wolfgang Sofsky, *The Order of Terror: The Concentration Camp*, trans. William Templer (Princeton: Princeton University Press, 1997), p. 229.

19. See the perceptive considerations in Bernardo Valli's article "Iraq, la guerra senza faccia," in the newspaper *La Repubblica*, 8 February 2006.

20. David Sussman, "What's Wrong with Torture," *Philosophy and Public Affairs* 33, no. 1 (2005): 7.

21. Ibid., p. 19.

22. See Mark Danner, "Abu Ghraib: The Hidden Story," in *New York Review of Books*, 7 October 2004.

23. A classic book on this topic, recently reprinted, remains George Ryley Scott, *A History of Torture Throughout the Ages* (London: Kegan Paul, 2003; distributed by Columbia University Press). See also Edward Peters, *Torture* (Philadelphia: University of Pennsylvania Press, 1996); and Michael Kerrigan, *The History of Torture* (New York: Lyons, 2001).

24. For the expression "interrogational torture," as well as "terroristic torture" (which I mention below), see Henry Sue, "Torture," *Philosophy and Public Affairs* 7, no. 2 (1978): 124–143. Note the year in which this article was published. Taking up the theme of torture in the same journal in 2005, David Sussman alludes to "interrogational torture" only in passing and ignores "terroristic torture" ("What's Wrong with Torture," p. 4). Evidently, after Guantánamo and Abu Ghraib, "terroristic torture" has become an embarrassing category.

25. See the section "Interrogating Detainees" in *Ethics and Politics: Cases and Comments*, ed. Amy Gutmann and Dennis Thompson (Belmont, Calif.: Wadsworth, 2005), pp. 60–71.

26. As Elaine Scarry argues in *The Body in Pain*, pp. 28ff., these ends, albeit programmatically announced, are in fact spurious.

27. See Danner, "Abu Ghraib: The Hidden Story."

## Appendix: The Horror! The Horror!

1. Hannah Arendt, *The Origins of Totalitarianism* (1951), new ed. (New York: Harcourt, Brace and World, 1966), p. 185 n. 1.

2. [The author quotes from the Italian translation of *Heart of Darkness*, *Cuore di tenebra* (Milan: Mondadori, 2000), without page references. I supply the corresponding passages in English from the text available at the University of Virginia Library's Electronic Text Center, etext.virginia.edu/toc/modeng/public/Con Dark.html. WM]

3. See Edward Said, *Culture and Imperialism* (New York: Knopf, 1993), pp. 19–31.

4. See Chinua Achebe, *Hopes and Impediments* (New York: Anchor, 1989), pp. 1–20.

5. Arendt, *The Origins of Totalitarianism*, p. 190.

6. [The Italian translation, *Cuore di tenebra*, makes a subtle mistake of emphasis here, translating "inhuman" with the Italian term "*disumani*," which would actually translate the English word "inhumane." Cavarero spots the discrepancy and changes the Italian rendering to "*inumani*," which does correctly translate "inhuman," recording the change in her note here. WM]

7. See Roberto Tumminelli, *Sterminate quei bruti* (Milan: Selene, 2004), p. 46.

8. See Olivia Guaraldo, *Storylines. Politics, history and narrative from an Arendtian perspective* (Jyväskylä, Finland: SoPhi, 2001), pp. 155–170.

9. [The author quotes from the Italian translation of *Under Western Eyes*, *Con gli*

*occhi dell'Occidente* (Milan: Mondadori, 1998), without page references. I supply the corresponding passages in English from the text available at the University of Adelaide Library of eBooks, ebooks.adelaide.edu.au/c/conrad/joseph/c75u. WM]

10. [The author quotes from the Italian translation of *The Secret Agent*, *L'agente segreto* (Rome: Newton Compton, 1993), without page references. I supply the corresponding passages in English from the text available at Project Gutenberg, www.gutenberg.org/etext/974. WM]

11. Elsewhere, though, "the last new principle of general destruction for the sake of ultimate good" is mentioned, but the problem lies exactly here, in this shift that reduces the destructive act to its purpose alone. [The author quotes from the Italian translation of *The Possessed*, *I demoni* (Turin: Einaudi, 1993). I supply the corresponding passages in English from the text available at Project Gutenberg, www.gutenberg.org/etext/8117. WM]

# Bibliography

Achebe, Chinua. *Hopes and Impediments*. New York: Anchor, 1989.

Agamben, Giorgio. *Homo Sacer: Sovereign Power and Bare Life*. Trans. Daniel Heller-Roazen. Stanford, Calif.: Stanford University Press, 1998.

——. *Remnants of Auschwitz: The Witness and the Archive*. Trans. Daniel Heller-Roazen. New York: Zone, 1999.

Al-Azm, Sadik J. "Il pericolo dell'islamismo." *Reset* 97 (2006).

Allam, Khaled Fouad. *Lettera a un kamikaze*. Milan: Rizzoli, 2004.

Améry, Jean. *At the Mind's Limits: Contemplations by a Survivor on Auschwitz and Its Realities*. Trans. Sidney Rosenfeld and Stella P. Rosenfeld. Bloomington: Indiana University Press, 1980.

Appadurai, Arjun. *Fear of Small Numbers*. Durham, N.C.: Duke University Press, 2006.

Arendt, Hannah. *Crises of the Republic: Lying in Politics, Civil Disobedience, On Violence, Thoughts on Politics, and Revolution*. New York: Harcourt, Brace, Jovanovich, 1972.

——. *Eichmann in Jerusalem: A Report on the Banality of Evil*. 1963. Rev. ed. Reprint, New York: Penguin, 1977.

——. *The Human Condition*. 1958. 2d ed. Intro. Margaret Canovan. Chicago: University of Chicago Press, 1998.

——. "Mankind and Terror." In *Essays in Understanding, 1930–1954*, ed. Jerome Kohn, pp. 297–306. New York: Harcourt, Brace, 1994.

——. *The Origins of Totalitarianism*. 1951. New ed. New York: Harcourt, Brace and World, 1966.

Arendt, Hannah and Herman Broch. *Briefwechsel: 1946 bis 1951*. Ed. Paul Michael Lützeler. Frankfurt: Jüdischer Verlag, 1996.

Arendt, Hannah and Karl Jaspers. *Correspondence, 1926–1969*. Ed. Lotte Kohler and Hans Saner. Trans. Robert Kimber and Rita Kimber. New York: Harcourt Brace Jovanovich, 1992.

Arslan, Antonia. *La masseria delle allodole*. Milan: Rizzoli, 2004.

——. "Metz Yeghern (il Grande Male): Memoria del male ed elaborazione del ricordo nella diaspora armena dopo il genocidio." In *La memoria del male: Percorsi tra gli stermini del Novecento e il loro ricordo*, ed. Paolo Bernardini, Diego Lucci, and Gadi Luzzato Voghera. Padua: Cleup, 2006.

Badiou, Alain. *The Century*. Trans. Alberto Toscana. Cambridge: Polity, 2007.

Bataille, Georges. *L'érotisme*. In *Oeuvres complètes*, vol. 10.

——. "Hegel, la mort, et le sacrifice." In *Oeuvres complètes*, vol. 12.

——. *Les larmes d'Éros*. In *Oeuvres complètes*, vol. 10.

——. *La littérature et le mal*. In *Oeuvres complètes*, vol. 6.

——. *Oeuvres complètes*. 12 vols. Paris: Gallimard, 1970–1988.

——. *Le procès de Gilles de Rais*. In *Oeuvres complètes*, vol. 10.

——. *Sur Nietzsche*. In *Oeuvres complètes*, vol. 6.

Bataille, Georges, Pierre Klossowski, Jean Hyppolite, Jean-Paul Sartre, et al. "Discussion sur le péché." Annex 5 in Bataille, *Oeuvres complètes*, 6:315–359.

Bazzicalupo, Laura. *Il governo delle vite*. Rome: Laterza, 2006.

Bernstein, Richard. *Radical Evil*. Cambridge: Polity, 2002.

Bespaloff, Rachel. *On the Iliad*. Trans. Mary McCarthy. Intro. Hermann Broch. New York: Pantheon, 1948.

*Biopolitica: Storia e attualità di un concetto*. Verona: Ombre corte, 2003.

Bodei, Remo. "Ragione e terrore: Sulla tirannide giacobina della virtù." *Il centauro* 3 (1981).

Bolaffi, Angelo and Giacomo Marramao. *Frammento e sistema*. Rome: Donzelli, 2001.

Bologna, Corrado. "Tortura." In *Enciclopedia*, vol. 14. Turin: Einaudi, 1981.

Bonante, Luigi. "Terrorismo politico." In *Dizionario di politica*. Ed, Norberto Bobbio, Nicola Matteucci, and Gianfranco Pasquino. Turin: UTET, 2004.

Bonetti, Noa. *Io, donna kamikaze*. Pref. Anselma dell'Olio. Rome: Iris, 2005.

Buber-Neumann, Margarete. *Als Gefangene bei Stalin und Hitler*. 1947. Reprint, Stuttgart: Seewald, 1968.

Burke, Edmund. *A Philosophical Enquiry into the Origin of Our Ideas of the Sublime and Beautiful*. Ed. Adam Phillips. New York: Oxford University Press, 1998.

Butler, Judith. *Gender Trouble*. New York: Routledge, 1990.

——. *Giving an Account of Oneself*. New York: Fordham University Press, 2005.

——. *Precarious Life: The Powers of Mourning and Violence*. London: Verso, 2004.

Calloni, Maria, ed. *Violenza senza legge*. Turin: UTET, 2006.

Campana, Stefanella and Carla Reschia. *Quando l'orrore è donna*. Rome: Editori Riuniti, 2005.

Cavarero, Adriana. *For More than One Voice: Toward a Philosophy of Vocal Expression*. Trans. Paul A. Kottman. Stanford, Calif.: Stanford University Press, 2005. Originally published as *À più voci: Filosofia dell'espressione vocale*. Milan: Feltrinelli, 2003.

——. "Politicizing Theory." *Political Theory* 4 (2002): 506–531.

——. *Relating Narratives: Storytelling and Selfhood*. Trans. Paul A. Kottman. New York: Routledge, 2000. Originally published as *Tu che mi guardi, tu che mi racconti*. Milan: Feltrinelli, 1997.

——. *Stately Bodies: Literature, Philosophy, and the Question of Gender*. Trans. Robert de Lucca and Deanna Shemek. Ann Arbor: University of Michigan Press, 2002. Originally published as *Corpo in figure*. Milan: Feltrinelli, 1995.

Céline, Louis-Ferdinand. *Voyage au bout de la nuit*. Paris: Gallimard, 1952.

Chakravorty Spivak, Gayatri. "Terror: A Speech After 9-11." *boundary 2* 31, no. 2 (2004): 81–111.

Chantraine, P. *Dictionnaire étymologique de la langue grecque: Histoire des mots*. Paris: Klincksieck, 1984.

Ciani, Maria Grazia, ed. *Medea: Variazioni sul mito*. Venice: Marsilio, 2003.

Clausewitz, Carl von. *On War*. Trans. and ed. Michael Howard and Peter Paret. 1976. Rev. ed. Princeton: Princeton University Press, 1984.

Collins, John. "Terrorism." In *Collateral Language*, ed. Collins and Glover.

Collins, John and Ross Glover, eds. *Collateral Language: A User's Guide to America's New War*. New York: New York University Press, 2002. Italian edition: *Linguaggio collaterale*. Pref. Roberto Cagliero. Verona: Ombre corte, 2006.

Curi, Umberto. "Alle radici del terrore." *Iride* 46 (2005).

D'Agostini, Franca. *Logica nel nichilismo*. Rome: Laterza, 2000.

Danner, Mark. "Abu Ghraib: The Hidden Story." *New York Review of Books*, 7 October 2004.

De Luna, Giovanni. *Il corpo del nemico ucciso*. Turin: Einaudi, 2006.

Derrida, Jacques. *Writing and Difference*. Trans. and ed. Alan Bass. 1978. Reprint, London: Routledge, 2001.

Dershowitz, Alan M. *Why Terrorism Works: Understanding the Threat and Responding to the Challenge*. New Haven: Yale University Press, 2002.

Ernout, E. and A. Meillet. *Dictionnaire étymologique de la langue latine: Histoire des mots*. Paris: Klincksieck, 1985.

Esposito, Roberto. *Bios*. Turin: Einaudi, 2004.

——. *Categorie dell'impolitico*. Bologna: Il Mulino, 1988.

Euripides. *Medea*. Trans. and ed. Davide Susanetti. Intro. Maria Grazia Ciani. Venice: Marsilio, 2002.

——. *Medea and Other Plays*. Trans. Philip Vellacott. Harmondsworth: Penguin, 1963.

Feldman, Thalia. "Gorgo and the Origins of Fear." *Arion* 4 (1965): 484–494

Flores, Marcello. *Tutta la violenza di un secolo*. Milan: Feltrinelli, 2005.

Forti, Simona. "Banalità del male." In *I concetti del male*, ed. Pier Paolo Portinaro, pp. 30–52. Turin: Einaudi, 2002.

——. "Biopolitica delle anime." *Filosofia politica*, no. 3 (2003): 397–417.

——. "Le figure del male." Preface to Hannah Arendt, *Le origini del totalitarismo*. Turin: Edizioni di communità, 1999.

——. ed. *La filosofia di fronte all'estremo*. Turin: Einaudi, 2004.

——. *Vita della mente e tempo della polis*. Milan: Franco Angeli, 1996.

Foucault, Michel. *Discipline and Punish: The Birth of the Prison*. Trans. Alan Sheridan. London: Penguin, 1977.

——. *Naissance de la biopolitique: Cours au Collège de France (1978–1979)*. Ed. Michel Senellart. Gen. ed. François Ewald and Alessandro Fontana. Paris: Gallimard/Seuil, 2004.

——. *Security, Territory, Population: Lectures at the Collège de France, 1977–1978*. Ed.

Michel Senellart. Gen. ed. François Ewald and Alessandro Fontana. Trans. Graham Burchell. New York: Palgrave Macmillan, 2007.

——. *"Society Must Be Defended": Lectures at the Collège de France, 1975–1976.* Ed. Mauro Bertani and Alessandro Fontana. Gen. ed. François Ewald and Alessandro Fontana. Trans. David Macey. New York: Picador, 2003.

Freccero, John. "On Dante's Medusa." In *The Medusa Reader*, ed. Marjorie Garber and Nancy J. Vickers. New York: Routledge, 2003.

Freud, Sigmund. "Medusa's Head." In *1920–1922*, vol. 18 of *The Standard Edition of the Complete Psychological Works of Sigmund Freud*, trans. James Strachey et al. London: Hogarth, 1955–.

Freud, Sigmund. "The Ego and the Id" (1923). In *The Standard Edition of the Complete Psychological Works of Sigmund Freud*, trans. James Strachey et al, vol. 19. London: Hogarth, 1955–.

Galli, Carlo. *Genealogia della politica: Carl Schmitt e la crisi del pensiero politico moderno.* Bologna: Il Mulino, 1996.

——. *La guerra globale.* Rome: Laterza, 2002.

Girard, René. *Violence and the Sacred.* Trans. Patrick Gregory. Baltimore: Johns Hopkins University Press, 1977.

Grillparzer, Franz. *Medea: Tragedy in Five Acts.* Trans. Arthur Burkhard. Yarmouthport, Mass.: Register, 1956.

Guaraldo, Olivia. *Storylines: Politics, History and Narrative from an Arendtian Perspective.* Jyväskylä, Finland: SoPhi, 2001.

——. "Le verità della politica." Introduction to Hannah Arendt. *La menzogna in politica.* Genoa: Marietti, 2006.

Guolo, Renzo. *Il fondamentalismo islamico.* Rome: Laterza, 2002.

——. *Il partito di Dio: L'Islam radicale contro l'Occidente.* Milan: Guerrini, 2005.

Guolo, Renzo and Enzo Pace. *I fondamentalismi.* Rome: Laterza, 2002.

Gutmann, Amy and Dennis Thompson, eds. *Ethics and Politics: Cases and Comments.* Belmont, Calif.: Wadsworth, 2005.

Heidegger, Martin. *The Question of Being.* Trans. William Kluback and Jean T. Wilde. New York: Twayne, 1958.

Heisbourg, François. *Hyperterrorisme, la nouvelle guerre.* Paris: O. Jacob, 2003.

Herr, Michael. *Dispatches.* New York: Knopf, 1977.

Hillman, James. *A Terrible Love of War.* New York: Penguin, 2004.

Hobbes, Thomas. *The Elements of Law, Natural and Politic: Part I, Human Nature; Part II, De corpore politico; with Three Lives.* Ed. J. C. A. Gaskin. Oxford: Oxford University Press, 1999.

——. *Leviathan.* Ed. C. B. MacPherson. New York: Penguin, 1968.

——. *On the Citizen.* Trans. and ed. Richard Tuck and Michael Silverthorne. New York: Cambridge University Press, 1998.

Jansen, David. *Graced Vulnerability: A Theology of Childhood.* Cleveland: Pilgrim, 2005.

Jones, Ronald. "Orrore e ritualità." *Intelligence* 1 (2005).

Juergensmeyer, Mark. *Terror in the Mind of God: The Global Rise of Religious Violence.* 2000. 3d ed. Berkeley: University of California Press, 2003

Jünger, Ernst. *Über die Linie.* Frankfurt: Vittorio Klostermann, 1950.

——. *Der Waldgang.* Frankfurt: Vittorio Klostermann, 1951.

Juzik, Julija. *Le fidanzate di Allah.* Intro. Roberta Freudiani. Rome: Manifestolibri, 2004.

Kantorowicz, Ernst H. "*Pro Patria Mori* in Medieval Political Thought." In *Selected Studies*, pp. 308–324. Locust Valley, N.Y.: J. J. Augustin, 1965.

Kepel, Gilles, et al., eds. *Al-Qaida dans le texte: Écrits d'Oussama ben Laden, Abdallah Azzam, Ayman al-Zawahiri et Abou Moussab al-Zarqawi.* Paris: PUF, 2005.

Kérenyi, Károly. *The Gods of the Greeks.* Trans. Norman Cameron. London: Thames and Hudson, 1951.

Kerrigan, Michael. *The History of Torture.* New York: Lyons, 2001.

Lara, María Pía, ed. *Rethinking Evil: Contemporary Perspectives.* Berkeley: University of California Press, 2001.

Levi, Primo. *The Drowned and the Saved.* Trans. Raymond Rosenthal. New York: Summit, 1988.

——. *If This Is a Man and* The Truce. Tran. Stuart Woolf. Intro. Paul Bailey. London: Abacus, 1987.

Levinas, Emmanuel. *Proper Names.* Trans. Michael B. Smith. Stanford, Calif.: Stanford University Press, 1996.

Lewis, Bernard. *The Crisis of Islam: Holy War and Unholy Terror.* New York: Modern Library, 2003.

——. *What Went Wrong? The Clash Between Islam and Modernity in the Middle East.* New York: Oxford University Press, 2002.

Liddell, H. G. and R. Scott. *A Greek-English Lexicon.* Oxford: Clarendon, 1968.

Loraux, Nicole. *The Experiences of Tiresias: The Feminine and the Greek Man.* Trans. Paula Wissing. Princeton: Princeton University Press, 1995.

——. *Mothers in Mourning; With the Essay of Amnesty and Its Opposite.* Trans. Corinne Pache. Ithaca, N.Y.: Cornell University Press, 1998.

Lucretius. *On the Nature of Things.* Trans. and ed. Martin Ferguson Smith. Indianapolis: Hackett, 2001.

MacIntyre, Alasdair. *Dependent Rational Animals: Why Human Beings Need the Virtues.* Chicago: Open Court, 1999.

Marramao, Giacomo. *Passagio a Occidente.* Turin: Bollati Boringhieri, 2003.

Marx, Karl and Friedrich Engels. *The Holy Family.* Vol. 4 of *Marx/Engels Collected Works.* New York: International Publishers, 1975–2005.

Mayer, Arno J. *The Furies: Violence and Terror in the French and Russian Revolutions.* Princeton: Princeton University Press, 2000.

Mortari, Luigina. *La pratica dell'aver cura.* Milan: Mondadori, 2006.

Morton, Adam. *On Evil.* New York: Routledge, 2004.

Nagel, Thomas. "War and Massacre." *Philosophy and Public Affairs* 1, no. 2 (1972): 123–144.

Nancy, Jean-Luc. *The Inoperative Community.* Trans. Peter Connor, Lisa Garbus, Michael Holland, and Simona Sawhney. Ed. Peter Connor. Minneapolis: University of Minnesota Press, 1991.

Napolitano Valditara, Linda. *Lo sguardo nel buio.* Rome: Laterza, 1994.

Neiman, Susan. *Evil in Modern Thought.* Princeton: Princeton University Press, 2002.

Nicoletti, Michele. *La politica e il male.* Brescia: Morcelliana, 2000.

Pape, Robert A. *Dying to Win.* New York: Random House, 2006.

Pastore, Alessandro. *Le regole dei corpi.* Bologna: Il Mulino, 2006.

Peters, Edward. *Torture.* Philadelphia: University of Pennsylvania Press, 1996.

Portinaro, Pier Paolo. "Genocidio." In *I concetti del male,* ed. Pier Paolo Portinaro, pp. 104–117. Turin: Einaudi, 2002.

Prezzo, Rosella. "Il corpo pornografico del guerriero." *aut-aut* 330 (2006): 13–28.

Pulcini, Elena. "Il bisogno di *dépense*: Pulsioni, sacro, sovranità in G. Bataille." *Filosofia politica* 1 (1994).

Reuter, Christopher. *My Life Is a Weapon: A Modern History of Suicide Bombing.* Princeton: Princeton University Press, 2004.

Robin, Corey. *Fear: The History of a Political Idea.* New York: Oxford University Press, 2004.

Rose, Jacqueline. "Deadly Embrace." *London Review of Books,* 4 November 2004.

Rousset, David. *Les jours de notre mort.* Paris: Pavois, 1947. Reprint, Paris: Hachette, 1992.

——. *L'univers concentrationnaire.* Paris: Pavois, 1946. Published in English as *The Other Kingdom.* New York: Reynal and Hitchcock, 1947.

Sacco, Leonardo. *Kamikaze e Shahid.* Rome: Bulzoni, 2005.

Safranski, Rüdiger. *Das Böse; oder, Das Drama der Freiheit.* Munich: Hanser, 1997.

Said, Edward W. *Culture and Imperialism.* New York: Knopf, 1993.

——. *Orientalism.* 1978. Reprint, New York: Vintage, 1994.

Saletti, Carlo, ed. *La voce dei sommersi.* Venice: Marsilio, 1999.

Salter, Lee. "Problems of Politics, Media, and Truth: The BBC's Representation of the Invasion of Iraq." *Critical Studies in Mass Communication,* forthcoming.

Salzani, Stefano. "La città dei martiri: Bios e zoe aionios." *Teologia politica* 3 (2007).

——. "Teologia politica islamica: Un approccio." In *Teologie politiche islamiche,* ed. Stefano Salzani. Genoa: Marietti, 2006.

Sanmartin, José. "Sentieri Jihadisti." *Intelligence* 1 (2005).

Sartori, Giovanni. "Illusionisti pericolosi." *Corriere della Sera,* July 24, 2005.

Scarry, Elaine. *The Body in Pain: The Making and Unmaking of the World.* New York: Oxford University Press, 1985.

Schmitt, Carl. *The Concept of the Political.* Expanded ed. Trans. and ed. George Schwab. Foreword Tracy B. Strong. Chicago: University of Chicago Press, 2007.

——. *Un giurista davant a se stesso.* Vicenza: Neri Pozza, 2005.

——. "El orden del mundo despuès de la segunda guerra mundial." *Revista de estudios politicos* 122 (1962): 19–36.

——. *Theory of the Partisan.* Trans. A. C. Goodson. *New Centennial Review.* msupress. msu.edu/journals/cr/schmitt.pdf. Accessed 2008.

Scott, George Ryley. *A History of Torture Throughout the Ages*. London: Kegan Paul, 2003. Distributed by Columbia University Press.

Sebald, W. G. *On the Natural History of Destruction*. Trans. Anthea Bell. New York: Random House, 2003.

Segal, Charles. *The Theme of the Mutilation of the Corpse in the Iliad*. Leiden: Brill, 1972.

Sémelin, Jacques. *Purify and Destroy: The Political Uses of Massacre and Genocide*. Trans. Cynthia Schoch. New York: Columbia University Press, 2007.

Salamov [Shalamov], Varlam. *I racconti della Kolyma*. Trans. Marco Binni. Milan: Adelphi, 1995.

Shalamov, Varlam. *Kolyma Tales*. Trans. John Glad. London: Penguin, 1994.

Snell, Bruno. *The Discovery of the Mind: The Greek Origins of European Thought*. Trans. T. G. Rosenmeyer. New York: Harper and Row, 1960.

Sofsky, Wolfgang. *The Order of Terror: The Concentration Camp*. Trans. William Templer. Princeton: Princeton University Press, 1997.

Sontag, Susan. *Regarding the Pain of Others*. New York: Farrar, Straus and Giroux, 2003.

Stern, Jessica. *Terror in the Name of God*. New York: HarperCollins, 2003.

——. *The Ultimate Terrorists*. Cambridge: Harvard University Press, 1999.

Sue, Henry. "Torture." *Philosophy and Public Affairs* 7, no. 2 (1978).

Susanetti, Davide. *Favole antiche: Mito greco e tradizione letteraria europea*. Rome: Carocci, 2005.

Sussman, David. "What's Wrong with Torture." *Philosophy and Public Affairs* 33, no. 1 (2005).

Ternon, Yves. *The Armenians: History of a Genocide*. Trans. Rouben C. Cholakian. 2d ed. Delmar, N.Y.: Caravan, 1990.

Todorov, Tzvetan. *Hope and Memory: Lessons from the Twentieth Century*. Trans. David Bellos. Princeton: Princeton University Press, 2003.

Toscano, Alberto. "Il fanatismo, da Lutero a Bin Laden." *Reset* 97 (2006).

Townshend, Charles. *Terrorism: A Very Short Introduction*. Oxford: Oxford University Press, 2002.

Tumminelli, Roberto. *Sterminate quei bruti*. Milan: Selene, 2004.

Valli, Bernardo. "Iraq, la guerra senza faccia." *La Repubblica*, February 8, 2006.

Vernant, Jean Pierre. *La mort dans les yeux: Figures de l'autre en Grèce ancienne. Artémis, Gorgo*. Paris: Hachette, 1985.

Victor, Barbara. *Army of Roses: Inside the World of Palestinian Women Suicide Bombers*. Foreword Christopher Dickey. Emmaus, Pa.: Rodale, 2003.

Volpi, Franco. *Il nichilismo*. Rome: Laterza, 1996.

Walzer, Michael. *Arguing About War*. New Haven: Yale University Press, 2005.

Weber, Max. *The Vocation Lectures*. Trans. Rodney Livingstone. Ed. David Owen and Tracy B. Strong. Indianapolis: Hackett, 2004.

Werfel, Franz V. *The Forty Days of Musa Dagh*. Trans. Geoffrey Dunlop. New York: Viking, 1934.

Wolf, Christa. *Medea: A Modern Retelling*. Trans. John Cullen. New York: Nan A. Talese, 1998.

——. *Medea: Stimmen; Roman; Voraussetzungen zu einem Text*. Munich: Luchterhand, 2001.

Woolf, Virginia. *Three Guineas*. New York: Harcourt, Brace, 1938.

Zolo, Danilo. "Le ragioni del 'terrorismo globale.'" *Iride* 46 (2005).